The Wild Prayer of Longing

Poetry and the Sacred

New Haven and London, Yale University Press, 1971

Nathan A. Scott, Jr. THE WILD
PRAYER OF
LONGING

Poetry and the Sacred

Library of Congress catalog card number: 72–140538
International standard book number: 0–300–01389–2

Designed by Sally Sullivan,
set in Linotype Palatino type,
and printed in the United States of America by
Connecticut Printers, Inc., Hartford, Connecticut.

Distributed in Great Britain, Europe, and Africa by
Yale University Press, Ltd., London; in Canada by
McGill-Queen's University Press, Montreal; in Mexico
by Centro Interamericano de Libros Académicos,
Mexico City; in Central and South America by Kaimon
& Polon, Inc., New York City; in Australasia by Australia
and New Zealand Book Co., Pty., Ltd., Artarmon, New South
Wales; in India by UBS Publishers' Distributors Pvt.,
Ltd., Delhi; in Japan by John Weatherhill, Inc., Tokyo.

To Ralph and Fanny Ellison
with enduring affection

Contents

Preface

The new theologians of the present time, whatever their affiliation (Roman, Anglican, or Protestant), have of late been nervously remarking a profound erosion of the theological terrain as the chief religious fact of our period. The choric refrain that comes from these harried divines speaks insistently of what Nietzsche was already darkly alluding to nearly a century ago—namely, a great death that, presumably, has occurred in the Courts of Heaven. It is, of course, an event by which the clerks of divinity are very greatly stirred up, sometimes even (as in the case of a certain young American who was causing a great commotion a few years ago) to the point of imagining what Lessing was long ago proposing in his Education of the Human Race, that God did Himself arrange His own withdrawal, bountifully bestowing it upon humankind as the ultimate expression of His prevenient grace. The readiness of avant-garde theology to set aside ancient commitments and to submit itself to the most drastic surgery has in recent years, predictably, made it a frequent target of secular irony. In the autumn of 1963, amid all the clamor then being provoked by the appearance the previous spring of John Robinson's little book Honest to God, the British philosopher Alasdair MacIntyre spoke sardonically, for example, in Encounter magazine of the "cheerful, even brisk, style" in which this Anglican bishop espouses an "atheistic" naturalism "fundamentally at one with Hume and Feuerbach, and at odds with Aquinas,

Luther, and Billy Graham." And what is acerbic in Mr. Mac-Intyre's response to the idiom and tendency of Bishop Robinson's thought makes a representative instance of the irritated impatience which normally characterizes the retorts that are offered today by their secular critics to radical theologians who are candidly attempting to release the people of our time from those forms of belief that distract men from what is truly central for the religious consciousness.

Given the special kind of exposure which is inevitably a part of his cultural position, it is no doubt the case that, whatever may be the extent of his learning, the professional apologist for religion does not ordinarily claim any considerable urbanity of manner or easy ordonnance in the way of systematic argument. So he is often perhaps not well shielded against sophisticated caviling. But it would be a mistake for those whom Schleiermacher named the "cultured despisers of religion" quickly to conclude, therefore, that they command an ease in Zion unavailable to the homo religiosus. *For the immense perplexity about ultimate matters which is everywhere a part of the human scene today ordains that he, whoever he is, who supposes that he can smoothly set forth what is decisive for his life in a series of clear and distinct ideas is a man suffering a great delusion. And however awkwardly the religious apologist may be felt to stutter and stammer forth his testimony, the significant service which theologians like Paul Tillich and Rudolf Bultmann have rendered our generation has been that of keeping in view the deep restlessness of spirit which persists even after the consolations of traditional supernatural religion have ceased to be efficacious. Indeed, even in an age in which wisdom is conceived in the terms of such men as Freud and Wittgenstein, it continues to be felt that one of the great sentences in Western literature is that which occurs in the opening invocation of Augustine's* Confessions*—"Our hearts are restless till they find rest in Thee." And we feel that one of the profoundest experiences of the heart is that which the Germans call* Sehnsucht *(nostalgia), which the French call* inquiétude.

*But what is this "wild prayer of longing" that issues from
our spirits even after the idea of the divine* pantokrator *has
lapsed into meaningless banality? It is, I believe, quite simply
a nostalgic aspiration for what Mircea Eliade speaks of as
"hierophany."*[1] *That is to say, we crave assurances and mani-
festations that our world, for all of its radical contingency, is
nevertheless shot through and through with holiness, with a
sacred reality. Even the most confirmedly secular sensibility
finds itself arrested by the question "whether we can [still]
rejoice with things, or whether [they are] simply inane."*[2] *And
the contemporary cultural scene is replete with evidences which
suggest that one of the principal issues of our age concerns
the possibility of the modern imagination finding its ballast in
a sacramental realism which is independent of the supernaturalist projections of traditional piety. To be sure, as Wallace
Stevens says, "We seek / Nothing beyond reality," and it is,
most assuredly, "the vulgate of experience" that claims our
commitment—*

*The actual landscape with its actual horns
Of baker and butcher blowing. . . .*[3]

Yet—as

*We keep coming back and coming back
To the real: to the hotel instead of the hymns
That fall upon it out of the wind.*[4]

*—our search is for the "fresh spiritual" that the world defines.
The Hipster tells us to be "with it," and all the new experiments of our period in psychedelic ecstasy and polymorphous*

1. See Mircea Eliade, *The Sacred and the Profane*, trans. Willard R.
Trask (New York: Harcourt, Brace and Co., 1959).

2. Henry Bugbee, *The Inward Morning* (New York: Collier Books,
1961), p. 138.

3. Wallace Stevens, "An Ordinary Evening in New Haven," in *The
Collected Poems of Wallace Stevens* (New York: Alfred A. Knopf, 1955),
p. 475.

4. Ibid., p. 471.

sexuality, in folk-rock festivals and millenarian communalism, in syncretistic mysticism and "anti-politics"—indeed, the whole burgeoning revolution of the new "counter culture"[5]— may have as their major premise the hope that, if the hymn that falls upon the hotel out of the wind is of no use, the hotel shall be found, however, itself to have a hymn within. One feels, wherever one turns in this strange, late time, that, beneath the flamboyance and antinomianism which are everywhere rampant, the prompting passion by which men are today coming more and more to be most deeply moved is a great need—in the absence of God—to find the world in which we dwell to be, nevertheless, in some sort truly a sacramental economy, where to be "with it" is to be "with" a sacred reality. We are, it would seem, a people whose most imperious desire is to win the assurance that Moses was given in the desert near Mt. Sinai, that the place whereon we stand is holy ground (Acts 7:33). For, distant as the metaphysics of the philosophia perennis *now is, we still want to be able to make (as it is said in the Consecration Prayer of the Anglican eucharistic office) "a sacrifice of praise and thanksgiving." And thus it comes to be that, even for those to whom the traditional language of liturgical theology is quite an alien tongue, the sacramental question remains a most pressing issue, the question as to what it is in the nature of reality that can be counted on finally to sanctify human existence.*

Now it is this question that I have wanted to bring into the foreground in this little book. I speak, of course, from the standpoint of one whose habit it is to think about "the fertile tug-of-war between the transcendent and the concrete"[6] in the terms in which the issue is presented by the literary imagination; and, though I risk something like a systematic argument in the second chapter, my main purpose is not so much to push

5. See Theodore Roszak, *The Making of a Counter Culture* (Garden City, N.Y.: Doubleday and Co., 1969).
6. R. W. B. Lewis, *Trials of the Word* (New Haven: Yale University Press, 1965), p. vii.

a thesis as it is to suggest how powerfully the strategies of art invoke mysteries and meanings that might otherwise elude our grasp.

I begin, in the opening chapter, by recalling the account that Erich Auerbach gives in his great book Mimesis *of the world-picture which was held by the traditional or the premodern imagination. In this connection, I stress the centrality in Auerbach's argument of the concept of* figura; *for, as he maintained, it was this notion which constituted the crucial theme of Western poetry and philosophy and theology in the ages prior to the advent of the modern period. The figural interpretation of reality did, of course, rest on the belief that, given its providential supervision by the divine Sovereign, history has such a unity as makes all persons and events belong essentially to one continuum; and thus any single person or event, it was felt, might be declared to be a* figura *of another, however great the intervening chronological distance, if the two persons or events exhibited some significant analogical relationship. But, more importantly even, figural thought took historical existence itself to be a* figura *of that occult reality belonging to the supernatural, for the world was conceived to be but a shadow of the Eternal. As I suggest, however, it is most especially in this crucial particular that modern mentality finds itself standing at a great remove from the figural outlook, for we do not ordinarily take the world to be a* figura *of anything other than or transcendent to itself. And the first chapter tries to offer some indication of how the history of* poiesis *in the modern period reflects this gradual decline and disintegration of the figural perspective.*

Yet, once the world is "defiguralized," once it is disengaged from that occult reality of which it is presumed by the traditional imagination to be a kind of veil, must it not then become something stale and distant and nowhere "charged with the grandeur of God"? And can it thereafter be conceived in any fundamental way to be invested with holiness? This, it seems to me, is the question that increasingly haunts us, as we con-

template the possibility that l'oubli des hiérophanies (as Paul Ricoeur speaks of it) may have entailed, as its ultimate cost, the disappearance from the modern universe of any sacral dimension at all. Indeed, as I suggest, it is a prodigious kind of search for sacramental reality that accounts for one of the more interesting developments being reflected now by much of contemporary artistic life—namely, the rebirth of "savage thought" (la pensée sauvage) that follows upon the decline of the figural imagination.

In the middle chapter of the book, by recourse to the immensely fruitful ideas of Martin Heidegger, I have undertaken to offer some indication of how a sacramental vision of the world may indeed define itself without resort to supernaturalist figuralism. Then, in the concluding chapter, I turn to the late Theodore Roethke, who is, in my judgment, after Stevens and Frost, the American poet of our time whose achievement —notwithstanding the great restrictedness of his imaginative range—is rivaled in distinction only by that of Robert Lowell and John Berryman. And my intention is to offer the poetry of Roethke as a large example in our period's literature of genuine "sacramentation" unencumbered by figuralist illusion.

N.A.S., Jr.

Acknowledgments

Portions of this material formed the basis of the Earl Lectures at the Pacific School of Religion in Berkeley, the Harris Lectures at Bangor Theological Seminary in Maine, the Charles Eaton Burch Memorial Lecture at Howard University (Washington, D.C.), the Bishop Slater-Willson Lectures at the St. Paul School of Theology in Kansas City, the Reinicker Lectures at Virginia Theological Seminary in Alexandria, and the Tuohy Lectures at John Carroll University in Cleveland—in the winter, spring, and autumn of 1970. I wish here to record my gratitude for the gracious hospitality of my hosts on these campuses, as well as for that of those who received me with such warmth at St. John's University in Collegeville, Minnesota, where I delivered a lecture in November of 1969 which was also based on these reflections. Nor must I fail to speak of a pleasant visit to Denison University in October of 1969, where my Goodspeed Lecture was devoted to the themes of this book.

I have in earlier prefaces also recorded my gratitude to my friend Jerald C. Brauer for his constant help and encouragement over many years. But this book goes to press at a time when, after fifteen arduous and fruitful years of presiding over the University of Chicago's Divinity School as its dean, he has chosen not to stand for reappointment to his deanship and to resume his professorial labors; so I want again to speak of my debt to him. In all seasons, he has offered fidelity in friendship and (in our professional relationship in the University of Chicago) such a warm and steady endorsement of all my efforts as has made "all the difference": indeed, to have served on the Chicago faculty since 1955 under an administration so humane as his has been one of the great blessings of my life.

Finally, I should say that I continue also to be grateful for the generous cooperativeness in all ways of my editor at the

Yale University Press, Wayland Schmitt, who has been unfailingly helpful since our relationship began in 1965.

For permission to use quotations from copyrighted material the author is indebted to the following publishers and agents:

A. P. Watt & Son, M. B. Yeats, and the Macmillan Company —for a passage from the poem "Politics" in The Collected Poems of W. B. Yeats *(Copyright 1940 by Georgie Yeats, renewed 1968 by Bertha Georgie Yeats, Michael Butler Yeats, and Anne Yeats).*

The University of North Carolina Press—for a passage from Richard Eberhart's verse play Devils and Angels, *which is included in his* Collected Verse Plays.

The Princeton University Press and Routledge & Kegan Paul Ltd.—for a passage from The Collected Works of Paul Valéry, *ed. by Jackson Mathews, Bollingen Series XLV, Vol. IV,* Dialogues, *tr. by William McCausland Stewart (Copyright 1956, by the Bollingen Foundation).*

Alfred A. Knopf, Inc., and Faber and Faber Ltd.—for brief passages from the poems "An Ordinary Evening in New Haven," "Esthétique du Mal," "To an Old Philosopher in Rome," "Sunday Morning," and "Tea at the Palaz of Hoon" in The Collected Poems of Wallace Stevens.

For permission to quote passages of the following poems from The Collected Poems of Theodore Roethke *the author is indebted to Doubleday and Co., Inc.:*

"The Light Comes Brighter," copyright 1938 by Theodore Roethke; "The Minimal," copyright 1942 by Theodore Roethke; "Root Cellar," copyright 1943 by Modern Poetry Association, Inc.; "Old Florist," copyright 1946 by Harper and Brothers; "Weed Puller," copyright 1946 by Editorial Publications, Inc.; "The Flight" and "The Shape of the Fire," copy-

right 1947 by Theodore Roethke; "Cuttings" and "Transplanting," copyright 1948 by Theodore Roethke; "A Field of Light," copyright 1948 by The Tiger's Eye; "Where Knock Is Open Wide," copyright 1950 by Theodore Roethke; "Bring the Day!" and "O Lull Me, Lull Me," copyright 1951 by Theodore Roethke; "The Wraith," copyright 1953 by Theodore Roethke; "I Knew a Woman," copyright 1954 by Theodore Roethke; "Words for the Wind" and "The First Meditation," copyright © 1955 by Theodore Roethke; "Fourth Meditation" and "The Sensualists," copyright © 1958 by Theodore Roethke; "The Abyss," copyright © 1963 by Beatrice Roethke as Administratrix to the Estate of Theodore Roethke.

And for permission to quote a passage of the poem "Frau Bauman, Frau Schmidt, and Frau Schwartze" from The Lost Son and Other Poems by Theodore Roethke (copyright 1948 by Theodore Roethke) the author is indebted to Doubleday and Co., Inc.

For permission to quote the passages cited above from Theodore Roethke's volumes the author is also indebted to Faber and Faber Ltd.

Legislation is helpless against the wild prayer of longing.

—From Herod's soliloquy
W. H. Auden, For the Time Being

Chapter One THE DECLINE

OF THE

FIGURAL IMAGINATION

It seems often to be assumed today by the specialists in *Zeitgeist* that the most readily available index of cultural tendency is that which is afforded by literary art; and, concurrently, it is often assumed that religious thought offers the darkest and least reliable intimations of what is decisive in the life of our modern Secular City. The former assumption is one that is now deeply a part of our common store of unquestioned axioms, for we live at a remove of about a hundred and fifty years from those German Romantics—such as Novalis and Herder, the Schlegels and Jean Paul—who declared poetic art to be the dictionary of a people's soul. However remote from contemporary styles of thought may be the oracularity which was characteristic of this German line of speculation, the essential status which it accorded to imaginative literature has long since come to be taken very much for granted among the broad generality of educated men. Journalists, politicians, various kinds of sociologists, and all those whose stock in trade is ideas (or ideology) of some sort suppose that the poet, playwright, and novelist bring us "news" about our age, and a news more directly stamped than any other by what (in Wordsworth's phrase) is "felt in the blood, and felt along the heart." The most essential inwardness of a culture is presumed to find in the arts of the word a kind of objectification which is nowhere else attainable in so vivid a form as that which literature presents. And thus the rhetorics of poetry and drama and fiction are conceived to offer a peculiarly apposite material for the diagnosis of *Tendenz.*

Religious thought, however, is normally considered in our time to represent a cultural marginality so extreme as to disqualify it for any kind of large exemplary role. The hucksters of popular piety and those few remaining relics who practice the mesmerizing pulpit oratory of an earlier day are occasionally noticed by social psychologists and accorded some small importance as symptomatic of one or another kind of "psychosocial" stress. But theology, as an enterprise of humanistic intelligence, is generally held at a very considerable discount, no matter how great a reciprocity it invites between itself and the other great departments of systematic thought; and thus it is not often deemed, as a cultural effort, to carry in any significant way "the tone of the center." Indeed, the tack which the English philosopher Alasdair MacIntyre was taking in the first of his Bampton Lectures at Columbia University in 1966 provides a nice example of what is in our period a widely prevalent point of view: as he contended, "what is primarily important [for secular intellectuals today] is not so much to make fresh moves in . . . [the] debate"[1] with Christian theology as to recognize how marginal this debate itself has come to be with respect to the major forums of modern intellectual life.

From at least one perspective, however, the theological project and the literary project may be seen to have followed remarkably similar lines of development in the modern period —so that, far from seeming to be on the remote edges of cultural life, religious thought may be considered, in its own recent history, to illumine what has been the destiny of the lit-

1. See Alasdair MacIntyre and Paul Ricoeur, *The Religious Significance of Atheism* (New York: Columbia University Press, 1969), chap. 1 (p. 3). The Bampton Lectures in America at Columbia University were jointly delivered by Alasdair MacIntyre and Paul Ricoeur in 1966; and, in their published form, the two opening essays are Professor MacIntyre's, and the concluding two are Professor Ricoeur's.

erary imagination and in turn to be itself illumined by that destiny. For, by virtue of their passage through essentially the same ordeal, both, together—the religious imagination and the literary imagination—may be found involved in a common attestation about the peculiar challenge which is presented by our own late stage of modern experience. That particular development which the life of the Word, in both its religious and artistic versions, has undergone might be said to be the Decline of Figuralism.

The term *figura* had already, by the time of Cicero and Lucretius, gained a certain currency in pagan antiquity, carrying the sense of "model" or "copy" or "image." By the time of Quintilian, it is apparent that the term had indeed begun in the first century to take on a distinctly rhetorical meaning, for, in the ninth book of the *Institutio oratoria*, it is being used as a technical term for those circumlocutions which we call "figures of speech." But the concept of *figura* quickly gathered a further range of implication once it felt the impact of the burgeoning Christian movement. This new meaning seems already to have been fixed by the time of Tertullian, who, in his polemical treatise *Adversus Marcionem*, speaks of Joshua as "a figure of things to come," since it was he rather than Moses who actually led the Israelites into the promised land of Palestine, just as it was the grace of Christ rather than the Law which led the New Israel into the promised land of eternal life. It was in this way that the first of the great Latin Fathers augured the kind of use to which the term *figura* was to be put in later patristic as well as in medieval thought, where its meaning came to be that of the prophetic occurrence which foreshadows things to come. And, indeed, what the term brings most immediately to mind today is that whole tradition in biblical exegesis, reaching from the Fathers through the medieval Franciscans, of viewing the events and characters of the Old Testament as anticipatory or *prefigurative* of the events and characters of the New Dispensation.

These early methods of biblical study, to be sure, have long since been dismissed by modern scholarship as so much "biblical alchemy" (the phrase, I believe, is Harnack's) because of their highly unhistorical and rationalistic character. Yet today —largely through the brilliant researches of the distinguished German philologist, the late Erich Auerbach[2]—we are aware that, far from being merely an archaeological datum of antiquity, the concept of *figura* presents us with one of the most crucial keys for unlocking that whole sense of reality which prevailed throughout the Western community almost until the advent of the revolution in thought and sensibility which we call the Enlightenment.

What Auerbach perceived, with a most remarkable clarity, was that the great deposit of that whole stream of thought constituted by the Judaeo-Christian tradition was a unique kind of story about the world and about the human endeavor. It was, as he recognized, not only a story about how the world began and how it should end, but also a story that did in effect propose a way of interpreting the significance of the entire process. The whole saga had its beginning with Creation, and it ran on through the calling of Israel as the Elect of God and the various proving ordeals to which the Chosen People were submitted. The climax of the story was Christ's Incarnation and Passion, the coming of the Messiah and the New Israel; and the projected denouement was Christ's Second Coming, the Last Judgment, and the New Creation. It was within the terms of this great drama that all the events of human experience were assigned their significance. Indeed, the distinctiveness of the Hebrew-Christian mythos lies in part in the openness to divine influence which every segment of the human

2. Auerbach's most systematic elaboration of the concept of *figura* is to be found in his long essay "Figura," which is included in his *Scenes from the Drama of European Literature*, trans. Ralph Manheim (New York: Meridian Books, 1959). His *Dante: Poet of the Secular World*, trans. Ralph Manheim (Chicago: University of Chicago Press, 1961), should be consulted in this connection; and so too should his *Mimesis: The Representation of Reality in Western Literature*, trans. Willard R. Trask (Princeton: Princeton University Press, 1953).

reality is conceived to represent. And thus it is no wonder, says Auerbach, that the great figures of the Old Testament, for example—such personages as Abraham, Jacob, Moses, David, and Job—have a kind of concreteness, a kind of directness, a kind of historicity, that their Greek counterparts do not have. For the Hebraic imagination was controlled by no impulse to segregate the noumenal from the contingent and finite realities of nature and history. In this it differed very emphatically from the Greek tendency which, even from so early a time as that of Homer, inclined toward dualistic conceptions of reality that posited a great distance between the quotidian and the radically significant.

It is in fact, as Auerbach argued, precisely this dualistic habit of mind that lies behind what, in the terms of mythopoesis, was the chief bequest of the Greeks to the ancient world —namely, the doctrine of levels of style. According to this doctrine, there are distinct levels of literary representation which are determined by the stations of life from which a writer draws his human materials. There is, ancient theorists held, a high style, as there is also a low style: the high style was believed appropriate for the heroic personages and sublime events of epic poetry and tragic drama, and the low style— which was essentially a comic style—was considered appropriate for realistic depictions of ordinary life and of the lower strata of human society. Any mingling or mixture of the two styles was thought to be a violation of propriety. As Auerbach reminds us, however, this whole doctrine of stylistic levels found no basis at all in the world-story of the biblical people, for there the whole of reality is considered to be penetrable by Eternity, and no man is thought to be untouched by the finger of God.

In, for example, one of the most memorable chapters of his great book of 1946, *Mimesis*, Auerbach invites us to contemplate the immense difference in basic sensibility which emerges when Homeric poetry and the literature of the Old Testament are juxtaposed. Homer was, of course, far removed from the hierarchical doctrine of the separation of styles which was later to gain almost universal acceptance throughout classical antiquity, but Auerbach rightly insists that he was very much closer to that doctrine than were any of the great poets of the Hebraic world. Homer, to be sure, was not afraid to mingle occasionally the realism of daily life with the sublime and the tragic; but the ordinary, commonplace, everyday scene in Homeric poetry is normally an idyllic and uneventful realm, whereas, in the Old Testament narrative, it is precisely in the realm of the domestic and the commonplace that the great tragic and sublime happenings occur. In the Homeric style, says Auerbach, "scenes such as those between Cain and Abel, between Noah and his sons, between Abraham, Sarah, and Hagar, between Rebekah, Jacob, and Esau" are simply unimaginable. "The sublime influence of God here reaches so deeply into the everyday that the two realms of the sublime and the everyday are . . . inseparable."[3] So, whereas the elevation of the Homeric hero is something steady and unshakable, the great personages of the biblical narrative, though they are "bearers of the divine will," are yet people "the pendulum swing" of whose lives is much wider: they may not only fall but fall to a very low degree. They are

> fallible, subject to misfortune and humiliation. . . . There is hardly one of them who does not, like Adam, undergo the deepest humiliation—and hardly one who is not deemed worthy of God's personal intervention and personal inspiration. Humiliation and elevation go far deeper and far higher than in Homer, and they belong basically together.[4]

This "realism" of Hebraic tradition gains its consummate expression, of course, in the New Testament account of the most sublime occurrence in the whole of the biblical narrative—the scene of which is not a magnificently appointed palace but a

3. Auerbach, _Mimesis_, pp. 22–23.
4. Ibid., p. 18.

lowly manger in Bethlehem and a lonely hill on Calvary. "In principle," says Auerbach,

> this great drama contains everything that occurs in world history. In it all the heights and depths of stylistic expression find their morally or aesthetically established right to exist; and hence there is no basis for a separation of the sublime from the low and everyday, for they are indissolubly connected in Christ's very life and suffering. Nor is there any basis for concern with the unities of time, place, or action, for there is but one place—the world; and but one action—man's fall and redemption.[5]

Now it was this "realism" of the biblical tradition, as Auerbach has shown, which was a chief formative power in the Christian culture of the Middle Ages and which enabled the medieval imagination, with an extraordinary ease and nonchalance, to find in the quotidian realities of the everyday hour a "glass of vision" into the ultimate mysteries. The quintessential case is, of course, for Auerbach the case of Dante; and Dante's realism, like that of the entire medieval tradition (as in the mysteries and moralities and various forms of literary narrative), is distinguished by the consistently "figural" character of his thought. That is to say, the Christian vision of God's providence as overruling the world from its beginning to its end enabled Dante and the people of the Middle Ages to take for granted the essential unity of the human story. The entire human enterprise had but one context: it belonged, all of it, to one great drama which began with God's creation of the world and which would end with Christ's Second Coming and the Last Judgment. Thus events, however remote they might be from one another in time, could nevertheless be conceived as belonging to one continuum. This meant that the past looked toward the future, that the present referred back to

5. Ibid., p. 158.

the past, and—since all time is eternally present—that any person or event might be discovered to be a *figura* of some other person or event, no matter how chronologically distant from each other the two might be. Just as Adam might be considered to be a *figura* of Christ, or Noah's ark of the Church, so the figural principle might also be found to be operative not only in the history of revelation but throughout the entire stretch of human experience. Anything, in other words, might be a "figure" of something else if some essential relation of an analogical sort could be seen to unite the two. The historical Virgil, for example, was a master of eloquence whose moral qualities fitted him for guidance and leadership; thus he could be taken by Dante to be a *figura* of such a poet and guide as might be counted on to lead the human pilgrim unto the very precincts of Grace. Or, again, that living girl whose name was Beatrice and the miraculous beauty of whose spirit the poet describes in the *Vita Nuova* could be presented in the *Commedia* as a *figura* of that grace which is itself "a light between truth and intellect."

The fundamental logic of figural interpretation would be misconstrued, however, were it thought to have entailed merely a form of allegorism. Although in figural thought one thing does, to be sure, represent or signify another thing, Auerbach reminds us that, in contrast to allegorical constructions, any genuinely figural account of reality is predicated upon "the historicity both of the sign and what it signifies."[6] There is always something abstract, and even abstruse, about pure allegory, for the literal meaning is the least important part of it: what matters is the spiritual significance which the imagery of the story is intended to adumbrate. But figuralism is always firmly grounded in the empiricist concreteness of actual experience. It

> establishes a connection between two events or persons, the first of which signifies not only itself but also the second,

6. Auerbach, *Scenes from the Drama of European Literature*, p. 54.

while the second encompasses or fulfills the first. The two poles of the figure are separate in time, but both, being real events or figures, are within time, within the stream of historical life.[7]

The second term of the *figura* is no less historical than the first, and the historicity of both is related to the spiritual significance being symbolized in a way that permits us to see historicity and spiritual significance as mutually dependent, the one upon the other.

The hermeneutic of figuralism not only implies, however, the possibility of one worldly event being interpreted through another; it also implies that historical existence itself is a *figura*. For history has the character of an interim between the First and the Second Coming, which is to say that the grand design of the Creator is not yet finished. Because it is under the eternal reign of God, history is an unbroken continuum whose unity makes it possible for events to point to and illumine one another. Yet all events are marked by a certain provisionality and incompleteness, for, while they point to one another, they also "point to something in the future, something still to come." Thus "all history . . . remains open and questionable."[8] Moreover, all events display a tentativeness which is consequent upon their being related to something that is dark and concealed, to something which has been promised but which is not yet present. The world is considered to be but a shadow of the Eternal and is, therefore, itself felt to be essentially a *figura* of an occult reality.

It is in these terms that Auerbach describes what might be called the traditional or premodern imagination that prevailed very largely throughout the West up to the Renaissance and that was not indeed challenged in any absolutely decisive way until the advent of the Enlightenment.

It deserves to be remarked, however, that figuralism carried

7. Ibid., p. 53.
8. Ibid., p. 58.

within itself a principle making for its own dissolution—a fact which Auerbach discerned with his characteristic trenchancy. Already in Dante he descried a foretoken of upheavals that were to come and for which Dante himself provided a kind of preparation. It was, of course, the poet of the *Commedia* who gave to Christian figuralism its largest and richest expression: it was he more than anyone else who disclosed how powerfully, and with what suppleness, the figural principle could order the immense multifariousness of human experience. Yet, though Dante's vision of human destiny was a radically eschatological vision and though for him the temporal reality of historical existence was "only *umbra* and *figura* of the . . . ultimate truth,"[9] he did, nevertheless, conceive history to be the medium of revelation. In this, he was consistent with his basic commitment to figural interpretation. Yet the immediate actuality of human existence was so brilliantly rendered by his figuralist realism that, in effect, he lent the figure a fascination which surpassed that of its fulfillment. The personages of the *Commedia* are, to be sure, set fast in an order which is under the rule of God, but so powerfully rendered are their earthly deeds and passions that the world beyond the grave becomes but a stage for the enactment of an essentially historical drama.

In, for example, the tenth canto of the *Inferno*, Dante and Virgil are "journeying along a secret track" among those flaming sepulchers in the sixth circle of Hell wherein the heretics and atheists are buried. All of a sudden, there rises up from one of these tombs a figure whom Virgil identifies as Farinata, one who had been a valiant leader of the Ghibelline party in Florence and who had died in the year before Dante's birth. He stands erect, "as if of Hell he had a great disdain"; and when he learns that Dante is not a Ghibelline but a Guelph, he recalls, with an icy hauteur, how he twice drove the Guelphs out of Florence. Dante reminds him, however, that

9. Ibid., p. 72.

on both occasions the Guelphs recovered from their adversities and informs him that they did finally prevail. On hearing Dante's news, Farinata's only reply is to the effect that, if indeed the Ghibellines have been ousted from the city, this is for him a greater torment than the flaming bed on which he lies. In this same episode, the conversation with Farinata is interrupted by the sudden emergence of Cavalcante de' Cavalcanti, the father of Dante's early friend, the poet Guido Cavalcanti. He anxiously and tearfully inquires after his son: "Lives he not, then, in the sweet air? / Does the sun's light not strike upon him now?" When he perceives Dante's hesitancy in answering, he takes that hesitation to mean that his Guido is indeed no longer alive, and, uttering not another word, he faints, falling backward into his tomb.

Now, as citizens of the Infernal City, both Farinata and Cavalcante are intended primarily to have a figural function in the design of Dante's poem; but the very logic of figural interpretation does, of course, commit the poet to a realistic depiction of his figure, in all of its existential immediacy. And, indeed, so poignantly does he render the earthly reality of these two human beings that it becomes itself the focus of principal interest, while the world of the Beyond is felt to be essentially a stage for exhibiting their human passions.

> Their earthly character is preserved in full force. . . . Farinata is as great and proud as ever, and Cavalcante loves the light of the world and his son Guido not less, but in his despair still more passionately, than he did on earth. . . . We cannot but admire Farinata and weep with Cavalcante. What actually moves us is not that God has damned them, but that the one is unbroken and the other mourns so heart-rendingly for his son and the sweetness of the light. Their horrible situation, their doom, serves only, as it were, as a means of heightening . . . these completely earthly emotions.[10]

10. Auerbach, *Mimesis*, pp. 199–200.

And throughout the *Commedia*—whether in Hell, Purgatory, or Paradise—Dante's rendering of his dramatis personae does so vivify the passions and endeavors of the earthly scene that, again and again, the figural form itself by far surpasses in interest its eternal position in the divine order, thus breaking out of its eschatological frame and taking on an autonomous life of its own.

So, for all of his commitment to figural interpretation, Dante did in effect, by the sheer power of his poetic artistry, confer a dignity on the human universe which offered an essentially new experience to the European imagination. With him, as Auerbach suggests, the image of man is by way of beginning to eclipse the image of God.[11] By the time of Petrarch and Boccaccio a distinctly new sensibility appears to be taking form, and by the beginning of the sixteenth century it has begun very definitely to displace the old figuralism with a new "sense of the self-sufficiency of earthly life."[12] A humorist like Rabelais, for example, in designing the comic adventures of Gargantua and Pantagruel, was clearly unconcerned to contain the multiplicities of existence within anything resembling the cosmological frame of medieval figuralism. Instead, through his outrageous joking and high jinks, his purpose seems to have been simply that of inviting his reader to regard the world as affording an infinite body of material for sport and play. Or again, such an essayist as Montaigne, far from being guided by the old figuralism, appears to have dwelt constantly in the element of "things":

It is in things that he can always be found, for, with his very open eyes and his very impressionable mind, he stands in the midst of the world. . . . But he guards himself against becoming subject to the law of any given thing, so that the rhythm of his own inner movement may not be muffled and finally lost.[13]

11. Ibid., p. 202.
12. Auerbach, *Dante: Poet of the Secular World*, p. 178.
13. Auerbach, *Mimesis*, pp. 294–95.

This was, indeed, his most abiding concern—the rhythms of his own interior life—and his constant endeavor seems to have been that of listening to the myriad voices within. And when one comes to Shakespeare, one can discern no substantial evidence of this consummate genius of Western drama having been in any way centrally concerned with man's relatedness to a transcendent reality. The great personages of his tragic theatre, for example, are, as Paul Tillich once remarked of the figures in Rembrandt's portraits, "like self-enclosed worlds —strong, lonely, tragic but unbroken . . . expressing the ideals of personality of a humanistic Protestantism."[14] The old figural imagination, which envisaged everything humanly problematic as finally resolved in the Kingdom of God, has here virtually disappeared altogether. There are occasional hints and innuendoes of some "brave new world," but what is decisive in the careers of Hamlet and Macbeth and Lear appears to be very largely an affair whose settlement belongs to this realm here below.

Nor did the seventeenth and eighteenth centuries bring any halt to the tendency which had begun to be deeply a part of Renaissance tradition, of abrogating traditional conceptions of human existence as vertically related to a transcendent reality. Indeed, this tendency seems to have become generally very much more emphatic in the period of Boileau and Molière, of Diderot and Voltaire, of Schiller and Goethe. Molière's theatre, for example, is oriented not by any notion of *figura* but, rather, by certain concepts of nature and reason and common sense. That most characteristic example of baroque theatre presented by the tragedies of Racine is a theatre committed, above all else, to the celebration of the inviolable dignity of the human spirit. The great protagonists of the French Enlightenment were, of course, dedicated to a most candidly secular outlook, quite as much so indeed as such an English counterpart of theirs as David Hume. And, in German tradition of

14. Paul J. Tillich, "The World Situation," in *The Christian Answer*, ed. Henry P. Van Dusen (New York: Charles Scribner's Sons, 1945), p. 10.

the late eighteenth and early nineteenth centuries, sentimental bourgeois drama and fiction, though often drenched in moralism, make up a literature moving always toward the expulsion of the Transcendent—like the somewhat earlier English tradition of Defoe and Richardson and Fielding, or the somewhat later tradition of Dickens and Thackeray.

So, by the early years of the nineteenth century, a climate of sensibility had arisen in which human life could be regarded as totally embedded within the objective system of historical circumstance and unrelated to any reality transcending the stress of temporal process. This new outlook first took definite form in the age of Goethe to which, of course, Herder also belonged, for he was a man of the second half of the eighteenth century. Yet it was to be Herder's destiny, through the posthumous influence of his thought, to teach the nineteenth century to regard history as a special kind of reality, a sphere of purely relative events all of which are woven into one general pattern and all of which are exhaustively explicable by reference to purely immanent forces. Herder was himself doubtless influenced in some measure by that strange genius of the early eighteenth century, the Neapolitan Giovanni Battista Vico, but it is from this brilliant German and his *Philosophy of History* that the modern idea of history ultimately derives. It was Herder who taught the modern mind to be cognizant of the problem of time, and he is a major source of that tendency to temporalize experience which marks the tradition of Hegel and Ranke and Taine and Marx. This was, of course, the tradition which, with the help of Darwin, prepared that ethos in the nineteenth century which formed the basic ambience of the new "realism" in literature—which was not a figural realism but the historicist realism of Balzac and Flaubert and the Goncourts and Zola.

Now it was this movement—the whole style of imagination represented by a Stendhal, a Balzac, a Flaubert, a Zola—to which Nietzsche planned to give large place in the book he was projecting just before the onset of his final illness, the book that for a time he intended to entitle *The Will to Power*.

For, in what he hoped would be the magnum opus of his career, he wanted to present a comprehensive analysis of that straitened condition of the modern period which involved, as he understood it, a total collapse of all values and which he called nihilism. And it was the advent of precisely this extremity that he found most powerfully expressed in the new Realism of the European novel in the nineteenth century. The way in which Nietzsche, as it appears, was prepared to regard such books as *Le Rouge et le noir* and *Illusions perdues* and *L'Education sentimentale* and *Germinal* may, of course, to some appear excessively overwrought and melodramatic; but one suspects that, in declaring this literature to be instinct with "the craving for nothingness," he was intending to challenge the assumption which pervasively haunts its pages—that the elemental human condition is not one of man's being in dialogue with the world, but is rather a situation in which man confronts a universe which is alien, in the sense of its being a system of objective facts or forces essentially unrelated to the human presence itself.

The usual textbook description of the theoretic outlook underlying the Realist canon emphasizes, and not incorrectly, the great new passion that took hold of the literary imagination in the nineteenth century for viewing the world as a vast collocation of "facts." Taine was, of course, the critic who deserves to be considered a major strategist of this development, and the lesson he was to lay down in his influential treatise *De l'intelligence* did not fail to make its impression— that (as he said in his Preface) "the matter of all knowledge . . . [is] little facts, well chosen, . . . amply circumstantiated, and minutely noted." It was a dictum delivered with an extraordinarily imperial kind of assurance, but it did so truly summarize the characteristic assumptions of the century that we may think of it as pointing not only to the kind of program undertaken by those who came after Flaubert but also to that which was being launched even by Taine's immediate predecessors. The genre most easily adaptable to realist doctrine was, of course, the novel; and Stendhal, in a book like *Le Rouge et*

le noir, was already committing the novel to facts, well chosen
and amply circumstantiated. The Balzac of *La Comédie humaine* was, clearly, a writer who conceived himself to be a sort
of secretary of his generation, one whose supreme obligation
was to compile and order the facts, the facts of manners and
politics—the price of bread, the styles of family life, the relations between a worker and his boss, and everything else
that might be a significant part of the daily round. The minute-
ness with which Flaubert rendered the details of ordinary life
—the ennui of a silly young suburban housewife, the dull
stupidity of her imperceptive husband, the drab banality of
their little backwater of a provincial town—convinces us that
such a book as *Madame Bovary* was surely a product of note-
books in which observed and fully documented facts were
carefully recorded. The Turgenev of *Fathers and Sons* would
appear certainly not to have been untouched by Taine's doctrine. And by the time of the Goncourts and Zola, the fascination with the fact had become a strict ideology requiring
the novel to be "a slice of life" and to specialize in what the
Goncourts called *reportage*.

What may now strike us as most significant, however, in
this whole effort to locate the true center of gravity for modern
consciousness in the fact, is the basic picture of experience
on which it was built. For the metaphysic of the fact does, of
course, presuppose that the normative human situation is that
of man's standing over *against* the world as that which is "out
there," from which he is separated, between which and himself
there is an ineluctable distance. When the world is viewed as
a world of *fact*, it is viewed as a theatre of reality from which
man is detached; the assumption being implicitly made is that
the human situation is *outside* what is called the "objective"
world. Since the human spirit is not included in the world and
the world itself is therefore something alien, it must follow
that there can be no engagement between literature and the
reality of the world unless the artist muffles his voice and sup-
presses his own personality to as great an extent as possible.
The world being at a distance from the writer, he must ap-

proach it impersonally and "scientifically": he must render rather than tell, he must give a stenographic report rather than any sort of formed judgment. He must, indeed, accomplish his own disappearance, in order that justice may be done the world "out there." And so Flaubert aimed at endowing his art "with the exactness of the physical sciences," and the Goncourts declared anything less than scientific exactitude in literature to be mere *anodin*. Zola—taking his cue from the theorist of medicine, Claude Bernard (as Balzac had taken his from the naturalist Buffon)—could see no reason why, if "medicine, which is an art, is becoming a science, . . . literature also [should not] become a science, by means of the experimental method"; so he declared himself to be a practitioner of what he called "practical sociology."

In one of his most memorable essays of a generation ago, "Three Types of Poetry" (1934), Allen Tate made an arresting proposal regarding the nature of Romantic Irony. It is, he said, "an irony of his position of which the poet himself is not aware" and which is a consequence of his revolting from Truth, as it is laid down by "the demi-religion" of modern positivism. That is, by deliberately embracing his own "fictions" as more congenial to his "unscientific" temper than the "certified" truths of a positivistic culture, the poet "defies the cruel and naturalistic world to break him if it can; and he is broken."[15] So Shelley falls upon the thorns of life and bleeds! —and then beseeches the west wind to waft him away and make him its lyre. Here, said Mr. Tate, is the very type and example of Romantic Irony.

Now modern Realism is not without its irony, too, and it is not wholly dissimilar from the Romantic variety. For, given the immitigable distance separating those two orders of being which Descartes denominated as "thought" and "extension," there is no achieving, finally, the kind of victory over the fact-world at which Realism aimed. No refinement of "scientific"

15. Allen Tate, *On the Limits of Poetry: Selected Essays, 1928–1948* (New York: The Swallow Press and Wm. Morrow and Co., 1948), pp. 101–02.

technique, no procedure of "documentation," no stratagem of *reportage* could, finally, establish the dominion of art over the recalcitrance of the so-called real world. And thus it did at last come to be that a Mallarmé made the other side of Flaubert's coin, a Proust of Zola's, a Rilke of Hauptmann's, a Pirandello of Giovanni Verga's, a Virginia Woolf of Arnold Bennett's.

This might be considered to be the Realistic Irony: the fact-world proving to be ultimately uncontainable within the framing structures of art—no matter how spaciously designed or scientifically precise those structures were made to be—the artist's decision came in the end to be that of denying altogether the hegemony of the external universe and asserting the primacy of what alone promised some possibility of confirmation and control, namely, the inwardness of the human interior itself. The declaration that is made by Mallarmé and Valéry, by Rilke and Stevens, by Joyce and Broch, is that reality is an activity of the spirit, that (if the language of William Blake may be used here) "This World of Imagination is Infinite & Eternal," whereas all else—"Generation, or Vegetation"—is "Finite and Temporal." Art is held to be (again in Blake's phrase) "the Tree of Life," and the poetic image is, therefore, conceived to be royally independent of the world's empirical givens, since the dark opacity of the world is an affair of "visionary dreariness." "The Imagination," said Keats in a letter (22 November 1817) to his friend Benjamin Bailey, "may be compared to Adam's dream—he awoke and found it truth. . . . Adam's dream will do here." Which is precisely the position of that line of modern writers stretching from Baudelaire through Mallarmé to Rilke and Stevens, to Joyce and Malcolm Lowry and Lawrence Durrell. In his dialogue *L'Âme et la danse* Valéry declared:

No doubt there is nothing more morbid in itself, more inimical to nature, than *to see things as they are.* . . . The real, in its pure state, stops the heart instantaneously. . . . O Socrates, the universe cannot for one instant endure to be only what it is. . . . The mistakes, the appearances, the play of the dioptrics of the mind deepen and quicken the world's miserable mass. . . . The idea introduces into what is, the leaven of what is not.[16]

And Wallace Stevens never tired of reminding us that, apart from this "leaven," there is nothing for man but "poverty":

> . . . How cold the vacancy
> When the phantoms are gone and the shaken realist
> First sees reality.[17]

To be a realist—merely "to see what one sees"—is, in other words, to dwell in poverty, because reality is "insolid rock," brutally fortuitous and irredeemably remote. So poetry is "the necessary angel"—that angel who, in disintegrating "the fictions of common perception,"[18] offers the only possible victory over a gaunt and barren world.

The acridly judicial tone expressed by talk about Fallacies in connection with the life of literature is no doubt not the happiest tone for critical discourse. Nevertheless, simply for the sake of verbal economy, modern literature may be said to have been chiefly guided by either of two principles, one of which may be called the Realistic Fallacy,[19] the other the Angelic Fallacy.[20] Under the dominance of the Realistic Fallacy,

16. Translated by W. McC. Stewart, in *Collected Works of Paul Valéry*, ed. Jackson Mathews (New York: Pantheon Books, 1958), 4 : 51–52.

17. Wallace Stevens, "Esthétique du Mal," viii, *The Collected Poems of Wallace Stevens* (New York: Alfred A. Knopf, 1955), p. 320.

18. George Santayana, *Interpretations of Poetry and Religion* (New York: Harper Torchbooks, 1957), p. 260.

19. The term is Erich Heller's: see his *The Artist's Journey into the Interior and Other Essays* (New York: Random House, 1965), pp. 89–98.

20. The term is Allen Tate's adaptation of Jacques Maritain's concept of "angelism": see his *The Forlorn Demon: Didactic and Critical Essays* (Chicago: Regnery, 1953), pp. 56–78. M. Maritain's notion of angelism is set forth in several of his books, but chiefly in *The Dream of Descartes* (New York: Philosophical Library, 1944).

the literary imagination conceives the world to be "out there," in its bare facticity, and that facticity is in no way felt to be itself a *figura* of any sort of radical significance. What man is understood to confront is a vast system of "reified" fact which is something alien and detached from *la présence humaine* and which must therefore be approached impersonally, with the impassive precision of scientific objectivity. So, for the sake of obedience to the fact-world, the artist undertakes the kind of asceticism that entails his attempting to eradicate the distinction between art and reality in order that all the "little facts" may be rendered with a proper carefulness and rigor. The aim of literary fictions is presumed to be that of "showing"—and perhaps even of suggesting a way of coping with —the hard, resistant, bedrock externality of the circumambient world. But, by muffling his own voice and banishing himself from his work, the writer only reinforces "the faceless hostility of the world and . . . [helps] to teach us that we ourselves are not creative agents and that we have no voice, no tone, no style, no significant existence,"[21] that we are simply automatons of the historical process.

The Angelic Fallacy works somewhat differently, for it springs from a profound disenchantment about the possibility of ever realizing what Realism seeks in its effort at mastery of the fact-world. Here, "the flesh of reality [being discovered] . . . too solid after all to be melted in the aesthetic fire,"[22] the artist elects, finally, to circumvent that solid flesh and make do with his Cartesian vacuum. He opts for some version of the doctrine that literary art should have nothing but itself in view, the notion which Baudelaire elicited from the poetic theory of Edgar Allan Poe and which, passing down through Mallarmé and Valéry, led to that whole modern experiment in what has come in France to be called *la poésie pure*. The writers standing in this line have wanted to create aesthetic

21. Lionel Trilling, *The Liberal Imagination: Essays on Literature and Society* (New York: The Viking Press, 1950), p. 270.
22. Heller, *The Artist's Journey into the Interior*, p. 97.

forms sufficient unto themselves, forms neither requiring nor tolerating reference to anything beyond themselves. They have insisted upon the essential gratuitousness of the literary act, and in their effort to be artists and *only* artists, they have often been like acrobats, inching their way along a tightrope stretched above a world for which they have no great love. The angelic mind—which rejects out of hand the too, too solid stuff of *things* and *facts*—wants to create a kind of absolute poetry that will in no way be dependent upon the received material of nature and history. Since reality, as Wallace Stevens believed, is itself an achievement of the mind's inventive ingenuity, one of "the creatures that it makes,"[23] he declared his conviction that "imagination is the only genius,"[24] the only clue we have to the human condition. And it is, in one way or another, a similar testimony that is made by the authors of such books as *Charmes, Duineser Elegien, Ideas of Order,* and *Transport to Summer; Finnegans Wake, To the Lighthouse, Nightwood,* and *Martereau; Ubu Roi, Sei personaggi in cerca d'autore,* and *Fin de partie.*

Now it is surely clear that a literature under the dominance of either the Realistic or the Angelic Fallacy is one which has been evacuated of anything resembling a sacramental vision of existence, for the decisive development to which it bears witness is the death of the figural imagination. In the one case reality is, in effect, declared to be wholly resident in the inert facticity of those public operables which are the material of empirical science. In the other case the locus of the real is conceived to be simply human subjectivity itself, man's dreaming and imagining and myth-making. What is presupposed by both styles of thought is that man faces a self-enclosed and unresponsive world which is not itself a "glass of vision": it seems to be without what Hopkins called "inscape," which is

23. Wallace Stevens, "The Owl in the Sarcophagus," *Collected Poems,* p. 436.
24. Wallace Stevens, *Opus Posthumous* (New York: Alfred A. Knopf, 1957), p. 179.

to say that our encounter with it is not felt to be an affair of seeing-*into* anything. It is not experienced as carrying within itself the power and radiancy of *presence:* it seems not to be ignited by any capacity for exchange or reciprocity. And, being without any numinous thresholds, it is beheld as something essentially dead—

> A heap of broken images, where the sun beats,
> And the dead tree gives no shelter, the cricket no relief,
> And the dry stone no sound of water.[25]

The figural dimension, in short, is gone.

Numerous young radical theologians on the American and the European scene have lately been creating a minor commotion by the excited flourishes with which they pick up Nietzsche's outcry of 1882 and announce that "God is dead." The language of their proclamations, to be sure, has often entailed a very extravagant kind of fustian whose effect has no doubt principally been bewildering for both the "religious despisers" of culture and the "cultured despisers" of religion. Yet it may well be that, for all of the high-flown excess and imprecision of their actual language, these harried divines really want to call our attention not to some tragic collapse that may be imagined as having taken place in the Courts of Heaven but, rather, to something which is immediately present in the cultural life of our time and which does indeed involve a kind of death—not so much of God as of the capacity, in the people of our age, for any kind of figural thought. For this, indeed, as the progress of imaginative literature most powerfully attests, is one of the decisive facts shaping human sensibility in our own late stage of modern experience—namely, the increasing difficulty that men have in thinking of the world as a *figura* of anything other than or transcendent to itself.

This realm of earth, it seems, can simply no longer be experienced as a veil for something else which is presently dark

25. T. S. Eliot, "The Waste Land," *Collected Poems of T. S. Eliot: 1909–1935* (New York: Harcourt, Brace and Co., 1936), pp. 69–70.

and concealed but which will ultimately be unveiled and made manifest. It is our historical fate to belong to a time in which, given the legacy we are bequeathed by the scientific movement of the past two centuries, men can no longer summon any serious belief in the doctrine that reality is constituted of *two* realms and that human life marks a point of intersection between *two* spheres, the natural and the supernatural, the temporal and the eternal. That premodern or traditional imagination which Auerbach described so cogently did, to be sure, apprehend the reality we meet in our common experience as a *figura* of some noumenal world of "the really real." But this whole way of responding to the human condition—what Rudolf Bultmann calls the "mythological" outlook[26]—survives now only vestigially. For its "linchpin" (as Bonhoeffer liked to phrase it)[27]—the doctrine of two realms which formed the metaphysical basis of figuralism—is no longer effective for modern mentality. And the insistence of much contemporary theology itself on this point suggests that the religious project has traveled a route very much like that traveled by the literary project and that there, too, the decisive development has been the death of the figural imagination.

It may well be, however, that we ought not to be in a great hurry to lament the passing of figuralism. Indeed, there is nothing in our modern experience of the world which would contravene the assumption that, given its manifest incapacity any longer to produce a cogent rendering of experience, it very much needed to die, if any real access to full maturity were to be won. For, as Francis Bacon realized at the very beginning of our era, man's learning how to deal with the plain, daylight

26. See Rudolf Bultmann, "New Testament and Mythology," in *Kerygma and Myth: A Theological Debate*, ed. Hans Werner Bartsch, trans. Reginald H. Fuller (New York: Harper Torchbooks, 1961), pp. 1–44. See also Bultmann's *Jesus Christ and Mythology* (New York: Charles Scribner's Sons, 1958).

27. See Dietrich Bonhoeffer, *Letters and Papers from Prison*, ed. Eberhard Bethge, trans. Reginald H. Fuller (London: Collins, Fontana Books, 1959), p. 91.

world of historical experience is contingent upon "Fancies, Ghosts, and every empty shade" being put to flight. Before he could assume full responsibility for his condition and destiny, he had to be liberated from captivity to the angels and principalities and powers which governed the life-world of archaic man. Indeed, as it was very powerfully argued by the distinguished German theologian, the late Friedrich Gogarten, the inner logic of the Christian faith itself required and to some extent sponsored the desacralization of the *kosmos*.[28] In one of the most ringing declarations of the New Testament, the apostle Paul announced in his Epistle to the Romans (8: 38–39) that none of the principalities and powers or ancient daimons can separate a man from God, since the guarantor of that relationship is now Jesus Christ. And it was just the consistency with which this testimony was made by the primitive Church which led their contemporaries to denounce the early Christians as godless men.

This, nevertheless, remained an essential Christian affirmation, that the new dispensation brought by Christ necessarily entailed a "de-divinization" of the world, since the great gift conferred by Christ was precisely the gift of freedom, of liberation from all the powers of darkness—in order that man, being now a fellow-heir with Christ (Romans 8: 17), might take on his primordially destined role of lordship over the whole of Creation. It was, of course, to be a long time before Christendom could begin to make any full acknowledgment of how much the essential logic of a Christian culture itself calls for radical secularization of man's relation to the world; even at this late date, Christian thought has not managed wholly to lay to rest the supposition that the proper alliance between Church and world is some form of heteronomy. But, whatever may be the confusions of the *arrière-garde*, the Christian faith, says Gogarten and many another theologian of our period, is unimaginable apart from man's being responsible

28. See Friedrich Gogarten, *Verhängnis und Hoffnung der Neuzeit: Säkularisierung als theologisches Problem* (Stuttgart: Friedrich Vorwerk, 1953).

for a world which, having been emancipated from all "principalities" and "powers," is a "de-divinized" world.

Considered from this kind of standpoint, the Christian faith is but a unique perspective—grounded in an historical datum: Jesus of Nazareth—on the reality of historical existence. There, if man is to "come of age" and step into maturity, he must find himself facing a world for which he alone is responsible, a world in which all the gods honored by archaic spirituality have been dethroned—a world, indeed, which, being independent of any *other*worldly plan or scheme of meaning, has ceased to be a *figura* of anything extrinsic to itself and is sealed off against any transcendental ingression from without.

But once the world, as it were, is "defiguralized"—once it is detached from that occult reality of which it was presumed by the archaic imagination to be a kind of veil—must it not then become an affair of taciturn blankness and inert facticity, something lusterless and distant, from the body of whose death the soul can only escape into its own inwardness? This may well be the fundamental dilemma of modernity, the issue which, in underlying everything else spiritually problematic for the people of the present time, is the fundamental religious problem of our age. It may also be that the uncertain inquiries which are nervously carried on today by theologians into "the crisis of theism" only represent a way, inconclusive and oblique, of talking about that unhappy sense which is so deeply a part of human consciousness in the modern metropolis—that the world (of subways and motorcars, of skyscrapers and revolving doors, of "ultra-intelligent" machines and urban anonymity) has somehow been divested of holiness, that no longer is it available on the terms of any kind of intimacy, that it is something stale and distant, "seared with trade; bleared . . . with toil," and nowhere "charged with the grandeur of God."[29] The term that has enforced itself upon us as most comprehensively describing our modern experience of the world is

29. Gerard Manley Hopkins, "God's Grandeur," *Poems of Gerard Manley Hopkins*, ed. Robert Bridges, 2d ed. (New York: Oxford University Press, 1938), p. 26.

alienation, and it is the condition which prompts something like that chagrined exclamation of Conrad's Kurtz—"The horror! The horror!"

We remember that monster whom we encounter in Dickens' *Hard Times,* Thomas Gradgrind, who is, we are told:

> A man of realities. A man of facts and calculations. A man who proceeds upon the principle that two and two are four, and nothing over, and who is not to be talked into allowing anything over. . . . With a rule and a pair of scales, and the multiplication table always in his pocket, Sir, ready to weigh and measure any parcel of human nature, and tell you exactly what it comes to. It is a mere question of figures, a case of simple arithmetic.

And, remembering Thomas Gradgrind—who is, to be sure, a man in whom the figural imagination is dead—we wonder if the world of twentieth-century life may not, indeed, be calculated to produce precisely this sort of "ultra-intelligent" machine and if there may not be something of Gradgrind in us all. For none of us is untouched by the kind of technological aesthesia which is epidemic in the Age of Computerization: we do all have it as our first impulse to suppose that whatever there is of contingency in the world is subduable by one or another kind of scientific engineering, for we apprehend the world as law, as necessity, as mechanism—as a system of objective and manipulable *fact.* And when we are reminded of our captivity to an order which, in being utterly amenable to control and regulation, is utterly faceless and therefore "alienated," we wonder how we may be delivered from "the body of this death."

Nothing, indeed, is more intolerable for man than being unable to descry opposite himself anything other than necessity, inert objectivity, faceless mechanism. When this is his situation, he is driven, by the whole logic of what it is to be man, to try to rehumanize his environment, so that it may once again be a world between which and himself some genuine reciprocity can be felt, a world in which he *participates* and in relation to whose life he is something more than merely an observer. This drive is primordially a part of the human thing itself: it cannot be set aside, and it is that which perhaps most basically accounts for the interesting development being recorded today by so much of contemporary literature and art —namely, the rebirth of "savage thought" which follows upon the decline of the figural imagination.

The term *savage thought—la pensée sauvage*—comes from Claude Lévi-Strauss, though his book of 1962 which bears this phrase as its title is by no means the first effort of a modern anthropologist to describe the fundamental processes and structures of primitive thought. Our eminent French contemporary inherits in this field a long and brilliant tradition of inquiry reaching back to American pioneers like Franz Boas, Alfred Kroeber, and Robert Lowie, and to Frenchmen such as Lucien Lévy-Bruhl and Émile Durkheim. What gives Lévi-Strauss' thought its immense distinction is not so much the novelty of his descriptions as the profound sympathy which he brings to the human adventure in primitive society. Indeed, it is this which saves him from the error (represented, say, by Lévy-Bruhl) of supposing that there is an absolute difference, in kind and quality, between the "prelogical" mentality of primitives and the "logical" mentality of those who are products of advanced or civilized societies.

The whole testimony being made by Lévi-Strauss in such books as *Tristes tropiques* and *Le Totémisme aujourd'hui* and *La Pensée sauvage* is in part calculated to suggest that, far from being prelogical or somehow unequipped for precise conceptualization, primitive man is in fact capable of highly rigorous thought. His thought may lack the kind of systematic and theoretical bias which characterizes the culture of advanced societies; it may often be an affair of what Lévi-Strauss calls *bricolage*, the sort of cognitive grasp of reality which is won by practical grapplings with the world—like the operational wisdom which a Thomas Edison or a Henry Ford achieves, not by any logic of the head so much as by a logic of the hand, of actual practice. Yet, though the empiricism of primitives may be a "science of the concrete" built upon such conceptions of causality as are congenial to the *bricoleur,* this "concrete" outlook, as Lévi-Strauss insists, is often capable of ordering the world with great sophistication and with great practical success. And thus, he contends, the primitive man's way of encoding his experience, however much it may be biased more toward concrete than theoretic forms, does in no way deserve to be conceived as prelogical.

But, of course, once Lévi-Strauss has been granted the point which he so powerfully establishes in this connection, the fact remains that the whole spirit and tonality of savage thought, if not prelogical, are nevertheless in many respects different from the characteristic tenor of our own thought. Lévy-Bruhl's description of that difference remains the classic account; though it may need revision in this or that particular, it continues at least in part to be corroborated by much of the controlled research of modern ethnography. His theory of the primitive mind is developed in various ways in all six of his major books, but the decisive statement of it is that which was presented in his famous book of 1910, *Les Fonctions mentales dans les sociétés inférieures.* Here the central notion is brought forward in the important second chapter, which is devoted to what he calls the "law of participation"; it is this, he declares, which governs the way in which primitive mentality conceives the relation between man and the world.

Whether we turn, says Lévy-Bruhl, to the Maoris of New Zealand or the Aruntas of Central Australia, the Melanesians of the Fiji Islands or the Negroes of West Africa, or indeed to any other "primitive" culture, the basic experience of the world will be found to involve a sense of man's participation in all the great realities, both animate and inanimate, into commerce with which he is brought by the adventures of life. Everywhere, primitive man perceives coalescence among the heterogeneities of experience, a kind of flowing wholeness whereby things are so fused into one another that distinctions between the one and the many, the same and another, the perceiver and the perceived, are not felt to have any primary significance. Things exist in relationship: they are members one of another. And since everything is felt to be instinct with vital powers, nothing is simply "objective." Consequently, there is nothing with which man may not stand in a relation of reciprocity, for everything shows itself to be charged with "presence" and open to dialogue with the human spirit.

When a man puts on the skin of a tiger and *becomes* a tiger, primitives "are not concerned with knowing whether the man, in becoming a tiger, ceases to be a man,"[30] for what interests them is "the mystic virtue" which makes both man and tiger permeable by and open to each other. Or in totemic communities, when, for example, the Bororos in southern Brazil boast that they are red araras, they are not saying that these parakeets are metamorphosed Bororos or that they themselves are metamorphosed parakeets, but rather that at one and the same time they are both themselves as human beings and these birds of scarlet plumage. Or again, when a North American Indian dancer declares himself to be a god, he does not mean that he is offering a dramatic portrayal of the god, but rather that his dance mimes his identity with the god, his participation in a certain divine reality.

And so it goes, Lévy-Bruhl maintains, throughout the whole breadth of primitive culture. Everywhere it is the law of participation which governs "collective representations"—that is, those symbolic forms which the primitive receives from his group for the ordering of experience. The phenomena of the world are apprehended as *Gestalten* which "give forth and . . . receive mystic powers, virtues, qualities, influences,"[31] and the relationships between the mystic powers of persons and

30. Lucien Lévy-Bruhl, *How Natives Think* (*Les Fonctions mentales dans les sociétés inférieures*), trans. Lilian A. Clare (London: George Allen & Unwin, 1926), p. 99.
31. Ibid., pp. 76–77.

things are conceived under the law of participation. Thus a
newborn child will feel the effect of everything his father
does; and the hunter's good fortune or failure will be dependent upon whether his wife, back at their camp, does or refrains
from doing certain things; and since a man's picture "participates" in his very life and is the human model, if harm comes
to the picture, it will come to the man himself as well.

Since participation is the universal law, the kind of natural
causality which preoccupies men in advanced cultures is of
secondary importance for the primitive. He is less interested in
immediate causes than in those ultimate causes that are rooted
in the unseen forces by which the universe is controlled. So it
is, in Lévy-Bruhl's classic account, that savage thought under-
stands the nature of man's contact with the world—as an encounter, it might be said, with that which is in every respect a
sacrament of "presence."

So deeply was Lévy-Bruhl captivated, however, by the
conceptions of progress and evolution belonging to the atmosphere of his time that he felt obliged to represent the
participatory mode of thought as a kind of prelogical mentality which man has gradually relegated to the discard in the
course of his steady improvement through the ages. And the
absolute contrast which his rationalist presuppositions led him
to insist upon, as between "primitive" and "civilized" thought,
is precisely that phase of his argument which now seems least
supportable by the ethnographic data gathered over the past
generation. For, as Edward Evans-Pritchard and Lévi-Strauss
and others have shown, primitive people may be no less adept
at rational thought and technological enterprise than we are,
their characteristic achievement in fact very often being a
readiness to make room in their cosmologies at once for objective, causal explanations of things and for "mystical" explanations. Nor, on the other hand, it is said, can the cultures of
advanced societies be considered to be quite so positivistic as
Lévy-Bruhl supposed, since the kind of cohabitation of empirical and "mystical" modes of thought discernible in many prim-

itive cultures is also frequently to be found there as well. So, as Professor Evans-Pritchard says, it is not so much at all "a question of primitive versus civilized mentality as the relation of two types of thought to each other in any society, whether primitive or civilized, a problem of levels of thought and experience."[32]

Indeed, nothing would seem just now more persuasively to recommend a relativization of Lévy-Bruhl's contrasts between primitive and civilized mentality than the remarkable rebirth of savage thought which begins to be a central development in cultural life today, on the American as well as on the European scene. Almost everywhere, one feels, the new avant-garde —in literature, in theatre, in painting, in music, in politics—is searching for ways of reconceiving the human universe as a world which offers the promise and possibility of life under the law of participation.

In a period when the arts ignite one another so quickly as they do today, it is difficult to locate just where it is that a review of the present cultural scene may be most fruitfully begun. For poetry and the novel, theatre and painting, music and the cinema are all in various ways being simultaneously influenced by currents of thought and vision that derive from such people as Alfred Jarry and Antonin Artaud, Kurt Schwitters and Marcel Duchamp, Samuel Beckett and Alain Robbe-Grillet, John Cage and Karlheinz Stockhausen, Jasper Johns and Robert Rauschenberg, François Truffaut and Jean-Luc Godard, Jackson Pollock and Willem de Kooning, William Carlos Williams and Charles Olson. The world of our contemporary literature and art is a whirling kaleidoscope in which painting may be seen to be a directive force in theatre, and cinema in fiction, and in which the numerous influences that relate one genre to another all appear to operate reflexively, so that the garment being fashioned by artistic enterprise appears to be without seams.

32. Edward E. Evans-Pritchard, *Theories of Primitive Religion* (Oxford: Clarendon Press, 1965), p. 91.

In a situation so volatile, where all the established genres are so deeply involved in one another's life that no particular medium—whether literature or painting or cinema—can claim a position of primacy, it may be that the basic impulse shaping sensibility today will be found disclosing itself with especial clarity in those forms of artistic expression which are most radically exceptional and innovative. This is at least an hypothesis worth exploration, and one phenomenon which it will certainly invite us to consider is that which initiates sometimes refer to as Action Theatre or Kinetic Theatre or Events, but which is more commonly spoken of as Happenings.

This new species of theatrical extravaganza was having a great vogue a few years ago in Paris and London and Stockholm, as well as in Chicago and San Francisco, so that it is not considered now (as at the time of its inception) to have any particularly close association with a special locale. But the essential plotting of the genre, and the coining of the term Happening, was at the outset the work of a young American, Allan Kaprow, a painter by profession, who, while teaching art history at Rutgers in the late 1950's, conceived a blueprint for an unconventional kind of dramatic performance. The first public testing occurred in October of 1959 in New York City on the occasion of the opening of the Reuben Gallery (on Fourth Avenue, just a block removed from Cooper Union Hall), when Mr. Kaprow presented his *18 Happenings in 6 Parts*. Almost immediately, it would seem, the form was felt to have an authentically contemporary kind of bounce and *élan;* and many other young impresarios of this new type of spectacle—often, like Mr. Kaprow, professional painters (Red Grooms, Jim Dine, Claes Oldenburg, George Brecht)—began to stage performances at the Judson Gallery and the Reuben Gallery and other congenial places in New York. During the period of the early 1960's, when the movement still carried the flush of novelty and when it had the fascination of a new cultural episode, a considerable diversity in styles of assemblage was, of course, a natural development, as many different talents were drawn into the excitement. And thus the term Happening now describes a broad spectrum of theatrical production. Yet the form has today an established character, and its protocol is easily identifiable.

A Happening might be defined as a type of theatre which uses a variety of media (music and mime and dance and films and readings) and which tends to employ only a very skeletal scenario, since it calls for much inventiveness of improvisation in its staff of performers. Its great purpose might be said to be that of compelling an audience to adapt to a situation which has been so arranged as to make it something strenuous and jolting and aggressive. The members of the "audience" may be herded into some network of dark passageways where flashbulbs are exploded in their faces, as bells are sounded and drums are beaten and two or three pieces of music are simultaneously blared out by phonographs, all this forming an accompaniment perhaps to messages of one kind or another being intoned by the performers. Or the events of the Happening may be simultaneously occurring in several rooms into which care has been taken to admit more persons than the available space allows for, so that, to see anything at all, one must fight for standing room, while perhaps having to endure being sprinkled with water or pelted with strange objects or required to exchange one's clothing with those nearby—and, possibly, being finally driven out of the hall into the street by a power lawnmower (as in Mr. Kaprow's *A Spring Happening* of 1961 at the Reuben Gallery).

Indeed, the Happening wants to be not so much a spectacle to be observed as an event demanding involvement. It is determined that a member of the audience shall not be merely a voyeur gazing at a performance, that he shall instead decide to give up in some measure the spectator's safety and really enter into an occasion, into some adventure in sensation and collective experience. Toward this end the scenarist may even prescribe certain actions for members of the audience, and the role he assigns his performing staff is one which entails most essentially what Michael Kirby, one of the chief theorists of the Happening, calls the "nonmatrixed" performance.[33]

The nonmatrixed performance is simply one in which the performer does not function within the matrix of any particular time or place or character. In traditional theatre, says Mr. Kirby, if, for example, the script calls for a performer to be shown sweeping a floor, a certain amount of character detail will be given: the actor will be sweeping vigorously or lethargically, carelessly or precisely. And he will "act 'place': a freezing garret, the deck of a rolling ship, a windy patio. He might [also] convey aspects of the imaginary time situation: how long the character has been sweeping, whether it is early or late."[34] But the nonmatrixed performer, since he is not functioning in any imaginary time or place and since he is not "imitating" an imaginary character, will simply execute the act of sweeping. It will not matter whether he "begins over there and sweeps around here or begins here and works over there," for his business is not "to create anything. The creation was done by the artist when he formulated the idea of the action. The performer merely embodies and makes concrete the idea."[35] And the Happening dispenses with the time-place-character matrices of traditional dramatic artifice precisely because it wants to abolish any distance between the performer and the spectator; indeed, the very distinction between performer and spectator is one which it wants to destroy altogether.

It is no doubt toward this same end that practitioners of the Happening reject the proscenium stage, putting on their shows instead outdoors—in parks or city streets—or in lofts or empty

33. Michael Kirby, *The Art of Time: Essays on the Avant-Garde* (New York: E. P. Dutton & Co., 1969), pp. 78–80. See also Michael Kirby, ed., *Happenings: An Illustrated Anthology* (New York: E. P. Dutton & Co., 1965); Mr. Kirby's long Introduction to this volume offers a systematic exposition of the idea of "nonmatrixed" theatre.

34. Kirby, "Introduction," *Happenings: An Illustrated Anthology*, p. 17.

35. Ibid.

stores or the basement boiler rooms of deserted factories, for limited audiences. For, like the practitioners of junk sculpture and action painting, they want to express a profound disbelief in "the museum conception of art"[36] and to create a theatre which sponsors a high degree of interpenetration between art and the world. Their lofts and stores are therefore designed to be "environments" filled with all the typical trash and débris of urban civilization—blaring radios and broken-down ice-boxes, cast-off commercial signs and neon lights, littered news-papers and girlie magazines, automobile tires and garbage cans. In short, the alchemy being performed is one which is calculated to make the spook-house of the Happening so thor-oughly coextensive with contemporary life that the theatrical experience, far from being merely an aesthetic encounter, will prove to be itself a deeper initiation into a world governed by the law of participation.

What the masters of these revels have done has been per-haps often very crude and bungled, sometimes undoubtedly vulgar beyond the limits of civilized tolerance. Yet many of those who in the 1960's experienced the best work of Claes Oldenburg and Robert Whitman and Allan Kaprow and cer-tain other scenarists of these new Events felt that exceptionally moving and incisive rehearsals of human experience were be-ing created—versions of what man's encounter with the world is now like that have a strangely bracing and renovative power. But, always, what was being aimed at was "total theatre" of a kind that invites more spirited and strenuous involvement in the reality that is today at hand for twentieth-century man.

For all of its novelty as a form of theatre, when viewed against the background of recent cultural enterprise the art of the Happening would not appear in any sense at all to be a phenomenon *sui generis*. Indeed, we feel it to have a certain exemplary significance precisely because it so much carries "the tone of the center" and gives the period away: it belongs

36. Susan Sontag, *Against Interpretation and Other Essays* (New York: Farrar, Straus & Giroux, 1966), p. 268.

unmistakably to the climate of John Cage and Merce Cunningham and Jasper Johns. In painting, for example, the decisive movement since the late 1940's has, of course, been Abstract Expressionism; and though artists like Larry Rivers, Jasper Johns, Kenneth Noland, and Frank Stella are today creating highly individual idioms that mark various sorts of departure from the programs of the early fifties, they stand in a line of succession that descends from Pollock and de Kooning and Kline and Rothko and are unthinkable apart from the major action painters of that period. But, despite the enormous variegation of the present scene, one thing is clear: the important painters today intend to extinguish the pictorial conception of painting and to put on their canvases "not a picture but an event"—namely, the event that occurs when the painter approaches his easel "with material in his hand to do something to that other piece of material in front of him."[37]

The New Realists, to be sure, have reintroduced—in the manner of a Rivers or a Rauschenberg—a recognizable subject matter, and they make large use of the materials constituting the ordinary visual environment of contemporary Americans (the Coke bottle, the drugstore hamburger, the slot machine, the supermarket). But the real function of these clichés is that of providing the artist with a challenge to explore the possibilities afforded by his assemblage for creating new excitements in the realm of structure and form. When you encounter in a gallery today a canvas by Pollock or Kline or Johns or Stella—which, all together, would make a very diverse group —it grabs at you with a strangely bothering kind of combativeness, demanding to know what kind of research *you* have conducted into the nature of our visual experience and, perhaps even by the very genius of its absurdity, asking how *you* envisage the world. It wants to destroy that "film of familiarity and selfish solicitude" (as Coleridge termed it) which ordinarily beclouds our vision, and it wants to invite us to make a

37. Harold Rosenberg, *The Tradition of the New* (New York: Horizon Press, 1959), p. 25.

kind of "sacrifice of praise and thanksgiving"—to run the risk of encountering the world under the law of participation.

Nor is it surprising, since so many of our younger painters have collaborated with the practitioners of Happenings and been deeply influenced (along with the latter) by the thought of the musical theorist and composer John Cage, that those currents of music stemming from his pioneering work should be found to be very much in accord with this whole ethos. Just as some of our painters have dripped their paint on canvas or hurled it from a distance, so Mr. Cage and his followers are greatly fascinated with aleatory forms in the composition of music, and the experiments in this mode of men like Sylvano Bussotti and Morton Feldman and Karlheinz Stockhausen represent what is perhaps the most radical employment of random procedures in artistic life of the present time. When these logicians of musical absurdity create scores which carry no stipulations regarding dynamics or pitches or time relationships —scores, indeed, carrying nothing more than whimsically drawn hieroglyphs which the performer is completely free to interpret as he pleases—their intention is to create a music which is no longer controlled so much by the composer himself as by the performer and the auditor, who are left free to conceive for themselves the imaginative "space" in which this music shall exist.

This intention is perhaps most especially revealed in the eagerness of these composers frequently to accord a high status in their designs to silence. When, for example, in Mr. Cage's 4' 33" the pianist simply remains seated for four minutes and thirty-three seconds before his closed piano, the "auditor" is in effect being told that the concert hall is under the law of participation, that it is up to him to create his own music. The declaration being made is to the effect that the work of art exists only in what Morse Peckham, in his elaboration of this doctrine, calls the "perceiver's space."[38] It is

38. Morse Peckham, *Man's Rage for Chaos* (Philadelphia: Chilton Books, 1965), p. 65.

something very much like this that appears, in the way of ideology, to be at stake in the kind of program that is often advanced today by the new insurgency in music.

That whole ambience which is so conspicuously instanced by the phenomenon of the Happening, though it finds characteristic expressions in music and painting and various other art forms, is perhaps most of all a consequence of radical movements in the literature of this century. It is, indeed, *literary* tradition which lies most immediately behind the dramaturgy of the Happening itself. The most proximate antecedent of Activities and Happenings is, of course, the Theatre of the Absurd, the theatre of Beckett and Ionesco and Genet, which forswears the illusionism of naturalistic drama in order that the audience, being confronted with a spectacle which is obviously not a literal reproduction of workaday reality, may be drawn into a new world where the distinction between theatrical artifice and ordinary actuality may be seen to be something extremely tenuous and uncertain. And behind the Theatre of the Absurd there are at once the "epic" theatre of Brecht and the scheme of Antonin Artaud for a "theatre of cruelty," both of which are premised on what Brecht called an "alienation effect"—namely, a complete annulment of the illusion that the Olivier on the stage is actually Hamlet, that Lee Cobb is actually Willy Loman. For, as both Brecht and Artaud profoundly believed, the theatre will never have any chance of changing a man's life until every last barrier between spectator and performer has been discarded, until the audience is drawn into the very center of the dramatic experience and offered something like a participatory role.

For the movement which most comprehensively sets the stage, however, for literary enterprise in this century we must look to Imagism—by which I do not mean that relatively unimportant eddy in the affairs of "the generation of 1914" with which we associate such minor figures as F. S. Flint, John Gould Fletcher, Hilda Doolittle, and Richard Aldington. I mean, rather, a kind of sensibility which provides throughout large areas of twentieth-century literature an example of what Marshall McLuhan calls "a mode of broken or syncopated manipulation to permit *inclusive* or simultaneous perception of a total and diversified field."[39]

There is, indeed, a strong tendency toward an imagistic rendering of experience which is noticeable in much of our century's poetry and fiction and drama; and when one turns to such representative masterpieces of the past fifty years as *Ulysses* and *The Sound and the Fury*, *To the Lighthouse* and *The Good Soldier*, *Paterson* and *The Pisan Cantos*, *Mother Courage* and *Waiting for Godot*, the principle that seems consistently to be at work is a principle of *collage* whereby the broken fragments of the modern world are brought into an adjacency which endows them with the power to become emotive images that reach toward some new design of health and happiness. The intention seems to be that the given poem or novel shall work like "those children's puzzles in which a lion or a rabbit emerges from nowhere when the numbered dots are connected in sequence."[40] By way of the excluded middle, this "art of radical juxtaposition" (as Susan Sontag calls it)[41] is calculated to register the writer's desire to create a work of art whose images are so fraught with the immediacy of the modern experience that the reader is lifted into a new intimacy with a world where it had seemed that things were fallen apart and the center no longer held—"that happy time," as William Carlos Williams said, "when the image . . . becomes a little fluid . . . [and] the rigidities yield—like ice in March, the magic month."[42]

39. Marshall McLuhan, *The Gutenberg Galaxy* (Toronto: University of Toronto Press, 1962), p. 267.

40. J. Hillis Miller, *Poets of Reality* (Cambridge: Harvard University Press, 1965), p. 145.

41. Sontag, *Against Interpretation*, p. 270. My application of Miss Sontag's term, it should be said, is considerably less specialized than hers.

42. William Carlos Williams, *Selected Essays* (New York: Random House, 1954), p. 307.

What is sought, says Williams, is "not 'realism' but reality itself."[43] In this characteristically blunt way the poet of *Paterson* makes a declaration—not only in his own behalf but also, as one may imagine, in behalf of a large body of modern witnesses—that neither Realism nor Angelism bespeaks a truth which is adequate to our human condition and that the world must somehow be found once again to be not a static universe of inert fact but an environment available on the terms of intimacy and offering the possibility of a participatory relationship. The great thrust of the imagination is toward that standpoint from which reality may be seen to be a thing of flow and dance, wherein things are charged with

> a kind of total grandeur at the end,
> With every visible thing enlarged and yet
> No more than a bed, a chair and moving nuns,
> The immensest theatre, the pillared porch,
> The book and candle in your ambered room.[44]

It is this drive toward rediscovery of a dimension of holiness in the quotidian that has so powerfully reinstated a type of "savage thought" whose most urgent expressions are to be found in many of the new artistic idioms of our period.[45] The inchoate yearning that seems to have captured many of the most sensitive people of our age, if given a theological formulation, might be said to be a yearning to behold the world as once again a truly sacramental economy.

Ours is, of course, a time, however, in which all the dualistic

43. William Carlos Williams, *Spring and All* (Dijon: Contact Publishing Co., 1923), p. 45.

44. Wallace Stevens, "To an Old Philosopher in Rome," *Collected Poems*, p. 510.

45. "Savage thought" not only finds significant expression today in the arts but also has its "theoreticians," the most influential of whom are such pundits as Alan Watts, Herbert Marcuse, Norman Brown, and the Norman Mailer of "The White Negro." These are people whose most immediate progenitors are no doubt the existentialists and certain European phenomenologists (principally, perhaps, Maurice Merleau-Ponty).

ontologies of traditional philosophy and faith have suffered an irreparable loss of cogency. For men who inherit the legacy of Hume and Kant and Nietzsche and Freud, the human experience is now, irreversibly, that of dwelling not in two worlds but in one; and Wallace Stevens speaks for the age when he declares, "We seek / Nothing beyond reality."[46] But when the nerve of "figural" thought has been thus impaired, is it any longer possible for the immanent givens of the world to be found bearing "coruscations of glory"[47] or in any way charged with the grandeur of God? If the two-storied universe of the premodern imagination is irrecoverable and if our present commitment is, ineluctably, to "things as they are,"[48] is it any longer possible for the world to be encountered as a sacramental economy, as tabernacling grace and glory, and as inviting orisons of praise and thanksgiving?

In full recognition of how much beyond redemption is the old cosmology of the figural imagination, the new theologies today often make brave declarations about what is called "secular transcendence," and they tell us that Grace is to be found in the midst of the Secular City, not in regions overhead. But is such counsel anything more than the verbal sleight of professional dialecticians? Does there still remain some large, real possibility that the world which is available to such people as ourselves can be experienced as indwelt by holiness and as therefore open to sacramental appropriation, so that the descent into it "beckons"[49] with the promise that we may join with all the creatures of the earth "in one / Multi-

46. Wallace Stevens, "An Ordinary Evening in New Haven," *Collected Poems*, p. 471.

47. Amos N. Wilder, "Art and Theological Meaning," in *The New Orpheus: Essays Toward a Christian Poetic*, ed. Nathan A. Scott, Jr. (New York: Sheed and Ward, 1964), p. 409.

48. Wallace Stevens, *The Necessary Angel: Essays on Reality and the Imagination* (New York: Alfred A. Knopf, 1951), p. 25.

49. William Carlos Williams, *Paterson* (New York: New Directions, 1963), book 2, section 3, p. 96: "The descent beckons / as the ascent beckoned. . . ."

tudinous oecumenical song"[50] in praise of Creation? This is the question which is being ever more urgently raised in our day; and the great resurgence of "savage thought" that follows upon the death of figuralism is but one evidence of a deep yearning to find the essential structure of reality to be a sacramental pattern which grounds our relationship to the world —to persons and things—in a dialectic of sympathy[51] and exchange. Like St. Francis of Assisi, we want to be able to address the sun and the moon, the fire and the water, the plants and the animals as "brothers" and "sisters"—and, most of all, we want to learn how to address one another more truly as "brothers" and "sisters." We want to find ourselves, in other words, not amidst dead mechanism but amidst a world which, in its every dimension, is under the law of participation because all created things are indwelt by grace and holiness and the life of God. And it is a kind of drive toward this happy meridian which is being expressed now by that whole contemporary tendency to which I have adverted here by Claude Lévi-Strauss's phrase, *la pensée sauvage.*

50. W. H. Auden, "Anthem for St. Matthew's Day"—which Mr. Auden composed to accompany the Litany for St. Matthew's Day that he prepared for the Church of St. Matthew, Northampton (England), for its Dedication and Patronal Festival (21 September 1946).

51. The idea of "sympathy" which is in view is so spacious a conception as that which was brilliantly expounded by Max Scheler in *The Nature of Sympathy,* trans. Peter Heath (New Haven: Yale University Press, 1954).

Chapter Two THE
SACRAMENTAL
VISION

The one term which, more accurately than any other, gives us the name for the way men increasingly live now, all across the face of the earth, is the term *metropolis*. In the very late stage of modern history to which we belong, we are, all of us, a people of the City, and the metropolis "is not just in Washington, London, New York, and Peking. It is everywhere"[1]—in towns and villages, in the East as well as in the West, and in virtually every corner of the human universe in our time. For, wherever men dwell today, they encounter the world as a structure of related regions and communities whose interdependence, being a creation of modern technology, does indeed constitute the metropolitan reality. The New Mankind[2] is an urban people, and the City—in its dense concentrations of humanity on large land masses, in its commitment to "functional" concepts of living, in its pervasive anonymity—defines the basic environment within which the various transactions now comprising the human adventure are carried on.

The traditional attitude of the religious community toward urban culture—toward its technology, its social mobility, its secularity, its flurry and bustle—has, of course, been one of

1. Harvey Cox, *The Secular City* (New York: Macmillan Co., 1965), p. 4.
2. The phrase is Gibson Winter's; see his *The New Creation as Metropolis* (New York: Macmillan Co., 1963).

mistrust and antagonism. On the American scene, this aversion to the metropolitan landscape has been so extreme that, in the case of the Protestant churches, the chief development over the past generation has been a great panic-stricken flight into the suburban areas surrounding our major cities. The intellectual vanguard in the religious community, however, has lately been submitting this whole tendency to a very stringent critique. Indeed, the new theology begins increasingly to be distinguished not merely by its declared congeniality toward the modern metropolis but also by the fervid enthusiasm with which it pronounces good precisely those features of urban life which have traditionally been offensive to religious sensibility—its fluidity, its rootlessness, its anonymity, its moral relativism.

The chief document in the case is no doubt Harvey Cox's ebullient and vivacious book of 1965, *The Secular City*, which, in its unflinching and delighted embrace of the metropolitan scene, stands as a major landmark of the new insurgency. Mr. Cox likes the mobility and impersonality of urban life and wants, as a Christian theologian, to celebrate the new opportunities that they bring for freedom and maturity. Life in the modern city, with its chaotic overcrowdedness and incessant turmoil of novelty, may, to be sure, be like a continual discothèque; but in Mr. Cox's rendering of the Christian sense of reality, the world itself is an affair of dynamism, of process, of openness. So he casts his vote for the metropolis, being untroubled by its secularity, since he believes that the whole deposit of Hebraic-Christian faith supports both a radical desacralization of nature and politics and such an awareness of what is relative and conditioned in the life of the human creature as entails an equally radical "deconsecration of values." In his wholly positive evaluation of a technocratic and secular civilization, this young American summarizes much of the testimony that has come from such distinguished European theologians as Dietrich Bonhoeffer, Friedrich Gogarten, Helmut Gollwitzer, Gerhard Ebeling, and Cornelis A. van Peursen

—which, allowing for the brilliance of Mr. Cox's own rhetorical gifts, is perhaps partly why, for a time, his book was so much at the center of theological discussion.

Mr. Cox is, of course, aware that his way of reckoning with the metropolitan reality is contravened by a substantial body of modern thought; but, in this connection, his tactic is one of imputing the status of cliché to the reports that for more than a hundred years we have received on the "dehumanization" that is suffered by the *Masse-Mensch* in the great cities of the modern world. It is, undoubtedly, a convenient stratagem of dialectic to dismiss as drearily hackneyed those conceptions which one's own system of thought cannot easily accommodate. But this is a procedure which hardly seems to be a wholly adequate way of responding to the very black view of the urban phenomenon that has come, say, from that great line of modern sociology running (crookedly) from Marx and de Tocqueville through Émile Durkheim, Georg Simmel, and Max Weber to Karl Jaspers, Ortega, and Jacques Ellul.

The tradition represented by such thinkers as these, though it conceives the metropolis to be our historical fate, is in no essential way controlled by any nostalgia for the imagined simplicities of the ante-metropolitan past. Indeed, it is, on the whole, affirmative of the pecular vitalities which are a part of urban culture, and it recognizes full well the deliverance from the smothering tyranny of "organic" communities which city life brings. But it is a tradition which, though appreciative of the gains that are brought by the rational planning and bureaucratic organization of the metropolis, also perceives the perils of "*over*-organization, [with its foreshadowings of] a future sterilized of the informal and the use-and-wont contexts within which personality takes on the stuff of resistance to mass-mindedness and cultural uniformity."[3] It is, therefore, a line of thought which issues, finally, in the kind of alarm that is to be overheard in the deliberations of Durkheim on *anomie*,

3. Robert A. Nisbet, *The Sociological Tradition* (New York: Basic Books, 1966), p. 297.

of Ferdinand Tönnies on the modern drift from *Gemeinschaft* to *Gesellschaft*, of Ortega on the new democracy of the "mass-man," and of Ellul on the hallucinated consciousness of the megalopolitan, who is a puppet of the technicians who run the city but who, believing himself still to be really free, lives in a condition of "anesthesia."

The vision of urban life projected by the literary imagination has been generally perhaps even more severe in its verdict than the report of empirical sociology. In 1819 Shelley declared that "Hell is a city much like London— / A populous and a smoky city. . . ." And it is a similar image that we encounter in the *fourmillante cité* of Baudelaire's Paris; in those "cold, wet, shelterless midnight streets of London" through which Dickens' Oliver Twist picks his uncertain way; in the dark, knotty maze of Dostoievski's St. Petersburg; in the "Unreal City" of Eliot's *Waste Land;* in the phantasmagoric underworld of Vienna in Elias Canetti's *Auto-da-fé;* in the bedlam and treachery that make New York a veritable nightmare for the nameless Negro who is the protagonist of Ralph Ellison's *Invisible Man*. The city, as it is rendered in literature of the last hundred years, is, to be sure, a place of opulence and celebrity, of marvels and opportunity; but it is also a place of loneliness and destitution, of crime and poverty—"a society in which there are no real equals, and no equilibrium, but only people moving *up* and *down*."[4] Its landscape is exhibited as a bleak and wintry labyrinth of brick and asphalt, of proliferating streets and alleys whose jumbled pattern is but a symbol of what is chaotic and disordered in the heart of the metropolitan himself. And the human polity is conceived to be an affair of people almost stiflingly bound to one another by the vast network of exchange and communication constituting urban life, yet divided by the immense distances that separate neighbors in a modern metropolis and that evacuate the very concept of neighbor of any truly human meaning.

4. F. O. Matthiessen, *Theodore Dreiser* (New York: William Sloane Associates, 1951), p. 75.

It often seems, however, that what the literary imagination finds most expensive in the urban experience is the city's enclosure of man in a world of artifacts, a world of his own creation in which, wherever he turns, he beholds nothing other than extensions of his own image. For, in this way, the city becomes a place of illusion and unreality: men begin to experience their own humanity as simply the product of the great machine of the social collectivity, and life everywhere seems to have the aspect of something gratuitous and arbitrary, for it seems universally to be a consequence of human artifice. In Wallace Stevens' "Sunday Morning," the lady who soliloquizes on a sunny porch over her late coffee and oranges one Sabbath morning finds the world to be, as it were, too thoroughly humanized, too drenched in our reality, too much the lengthened shadow of our existence; and she wonders if it is the same with things in Paradise, if

> they . . . wear our colors there,
> The silken weavings of our afternoons,
> And pick the strings of our insipid lutes![5]

It is a similar anxiety that the life of the modern city breeds in Ezra Pound and William Carlos Williams and Theodore Roethke and Saul Bellow. One might borrow a fine figure of Northrop Frye's and say that, to these and many other writers of our period, the urban experience seems often to be like an interminable railway journey in the course of which, as twilight and evening gradually darken the swiftly passing landscape, "many of the objects that appear to be outside [the windowpane prove, on re-examination, to be] . . . actually reflections of what is in the carriage," so that, once darkness fully settles down, "one enters a narcissistic world, where, except for a few lights here and there, we can see only the reflection of where we are."[6]

5. Wallace Stevens, "Sunday Morning," *The Collected Poems of Wallace Stevens* (New York: Alfred A. Knopf, 1955), p. 69.
6. Northrop Frye, *The Modern Century* (Toronto: Oxford University Press, 1967), p. 28.

Now it is doubtless this ennui of the human, which is so deeply a part of the metropolitan reality, that accounts for the deep yearning that appears to be felt by many of the most sensitive people of our age, most especially among the young —the yearning (as it would have been phrased by Martin Buber) to find "the speech of God" in some way articulated in the world in which we live and move and have our being. Amidst the culture of the city, everything appears besmudged by the human: nothing in the world seems capable of existing except by way of some form of human intentionality. And thus the sensibility of men living in such an environment comes to be stirred by a great need to descry some "otherness" in reality which cannot be made wholly subservient to the human project. But it will not suffice to find this otherness to be nothing more than the taciturn neutrality of objective fact, the inert blankness of "fixities and definites." For we want to be able to say something more about the world than G. E. Moore was prepared to allow when, as a kind of motto for his own philosophy, he took over Bishop Butler's proposition that "everything is what it is and not another thing." A certain kind of positivist astigmatism does, it is true, make for such a banalization of the world, as if it were merely an affair of inert facticity, merely what it is and not another thing. But, finally, there is no abrogating the primordial drive of the human spirit to find opposite itself an otherness which is available on the terms of intimacy, which is under the law of participation, and whose rhythms join our own mortal music to make some true counterpoint.

We covet a relationship to all the things and creatures of the earth that is grounded in a dialectic of reciprocity, of exchange, of love; and it is precisely the urgency of this yearning which is the prompting force behind many of the strange, new idioms in the literature and art and politics of the present time. The deracinated metropolitan wants again (as I remarked at the end of the previous chapter) to find himself living not amidst inert and faceless mechanism but amidst a world which, in its every dimension, is under the law of participation because all created things are indwelt by grace and by holiness. Indeed, the drama which is often being enacted today in the aesthetic as well as in the political realm is one which involves as its central action a violently strident kind of affirmation that the world is in truth essentially a sacramental economy. And thus it comes to be—most especially for those who would secure a sympathetic perspective on the literary imagination of our period—that the day's agendum entails rethinking what in fact it means to conceive experience sacramentally.

The region of meaning which is covered by the term *sacrament* may at first seem indistinct and elusive, for there is an immense variousness of conception in the history of religion regarding those actions and realities which may be thought to be conduits of sacredness. Yet, for all of this diversity, there is a certain persistently central assumption that appears always to have been made by those who have conceived the world to be in some sense a sacramental universe. We may call it the sacramental principle, and it makes quite a simple proposition —namely, that certain objects or actions or words or places belonging to the ordinary spheres of life may convey to us a unique illumination of the whole mystery of our existence, because in these actions and realities (to use Rudolf Otto's famous term) something "numinous"[7] is resident, something holy and gracious.

The traditional definition of a sacrament offered by Catholic Christianity is succinctly expressed in the Anglican Catechism, where it is spoken of as "an outward and visible sign of an inward and spiritual grace." This makes a serviceable formula not only for Christian sacramentalism but for the sacramental principle as it is generally to be encountered in the life of religion. For, wherever man's encounter with the world is interpreted sacramentally—whether among the Hebrews of ancient Israel or the Yoruba tribesmen of West Africa or the contemplatives of a Christian monastic foundation—there

7. See Rudolf Otto, *The Idea of the Holy,* trans. John W. Harvey (London: Oxford University Press, 1923), chaps. 2–5.

is some finite reality, some concrete, material sign, which is believed to be a vehicle bearing a special capacity to focalize what is Radically Significant and to convey "an inward and spiritual grace."

In, for example, the world of Christian faith and practice, bread and wine—the plainest possible symbols of our common life—are the oblations which are placed upon the altar as the supreme sacrament of glory. This is an action which Jesus Himself enjoined upon His disciples, ordaining that He should forever be "remembered" by the observance of a Supper. And one supposes that He chose bread and wine as the chief vehicles of this act of recollection because, since they must both be made and are therefore the fruit of man's labor, they are nicely fitted to be outward symbols not only of the grace which is resident in the created world but also of ourselves. For the Christian man, in placing bread and wine upon the altar, is in effect offering and presenting himself as a living sacrifice of praise and thanksgiving unto God.

When the oblations have been laid upon the altar, they are "consecrated"—which is to say that the president of the rite leads the assembled people in a great prayer of thanksgiving for all the blessings of this life and, most especially, for the supreme blessing of Christ Himself; and the Prayer of Consecration also pleads that the oblations may be so hallowed as to become what Christ did promise that this Supper would be, namely, a way of entering into His life and into His mission in the world. So it is that the Christian Eucharist goes, and it is the Church's faith that, once the Prayer of Consecration has been rightly offered, *our* offering is made one with *His* offering, so that He is Himself verily present in the bread and the wine—so much so that, by receiving them, we do indeed ourselves enter into the manhood of Him who was God's own figuration of the true and perfect man. "So we, being many, are one body in Christ, and every one members one of another" (Romans 12: 5).

This might be said to be the essential "logic" of what Christians variously call the Mass or the Eucharist, the Lord's

Supper or the Divine Liturgy. And it is this supreme sacrament of the Christian faith which, perhaps more clearly than any other, illumines the essential genius of the sacramental principle, namely, its power to break down all partitions between the sacred and the quotidian. For in the very ordinariness of the elements which the Eucharist employs—things so simple as food and drink—we may see something of how radically secular is the approach which the sacramental imagination makes to the world. That is to say, it is not concerned with any special world of sacred things that is conceived to stand over against the commonplace and the everyday; on the contrary, it has a lively vision of the sacredness of the commonplace, and it finds what is sufficient unto salvation in the homeliest experience of our daily round—the breaking of bread and the sharing of wine.

The bread that is broken at a Christian altar is, however, not truly broken unless other bread is broken for the hungry and shared with men of every race and color: otherwise, the communicants simply invoke upon themselves the "judgment" of Christ and deny what they are obliged to affirm—the essential congruence between the Liturgy and the common life. But not only does the Eucharist carry in this way a powerfully prophetic ethical implication; it carries also an equally significant ontological implication. For bread and wine could not be set apart for consecration unless ours were in some basic sense a sacramental universe and unless rivers and trees and tractors and spinning wheels were also eligible to be considered as "sacramentals."[8] And thus one of the most searching questions posed by the sacramental principle concerns what general perspective on reality it may be under which the world, in its every aspect, can be found to be itself something essentially sacramental.

That *theoria* of reality which is known as the *philosophia perennis* has traditionally answered this question by declaring,

8. See Joseph Fletcher, *William Temple* (New York: Seabury Press, 1960), p. 93; also Donald M. Baillie, *The Theology of the Sacraments* (London: Faber and Faber, 1957), pp. 42–47.

in effect, that the sacramental character of existence is established by the immanence within our restlessly changing and transient universe of an immutable, impassive, immaterial, self-subsistent Being, the *ens realissimum*, the *Actus Purus*. This supreme Being is the *deus faber*,[9] who created the world and who bears toward it something of the same kind of relation that a poet bears toward his poem. Just as Dante's *Commedia* or Wordsworth's *Prelude* may be considered, in all its facets, to be an expression of the mind and nature of the poet —with the poet himself, therefore, immanent within his poem —so the entire universe, on both its spiritual and material levels, is declared by the *philosophia perennis* to be the self-expression of the *deus faber*. And therein, we are told, resides its sacramental quality: in its derivation from, its dependence upon, and its reflection of the Divine Maker. It is the *machina ex deo*.

For all of the immense subtlety which has been a part of the great expositions of classical theism, there is a long tradition of modern criticism which has insisted upon the essential incoherence of this whole structure of thought. Indeed, the cardinal notion of some sort of immaterial Person behind the myriad phenomena of experience has today died the death of so many qualifications that vast numbers of people are, in effect, prepared to make a confession something like that made a hundred and fifty years ago by the French astronomer Laplace, when he said: "I have no need of that hypothesis." As Dietrich Bonhoeffer said in his typically blunt and straightforward way, the people of the modern period have simply "learned to cope with all questions of importance without recourse to God as a working hypothesis."[10] Men whose sense of reality is determined, among other things, by cybernetics and space travel and the physics of fundamental particles find the

---

9. The term is Alan Watts's: see his *Beyond Theology: The Art of Godmanship* (New York: Pantheon Books, 1964), p. 63.

10. Dietrich Bonhoeffer, *Letters and Papers from Prison*, ed. Eberhard Bethge, trans. Reginald H. Fuller (London: Collins, Fontana Books, 1959), pp. 106–07.

meaning of the word God to be so shadowy, so elusive, so ineffable, that atheism itself has virtually ceased to be a vital movement in the cultural forums of our time, and the kind of passionate disavowal that was still being expressed, say, a generation ago by Bertrand Russell in his once-famous statement on "A Free Man's Worship" seems today to belong to a very distant past.

We take it for granted now that language functions intelligibly only when it sets forth how matters are in a world made up exclusively of things and our human neighbors, and so habituated are we in the assumption that we dwell not in two worlds but in one that no longer is there any inclination even to assert this in a contentious and polemical way. In the setting of a metropolitan and technological culture, our whole experience of the world in no way suggests that human life marks some point of intersection between Nature and Supernature. The old supernaturalist postulates of classical theism are simply no longer felt along our pulses, and thus the question as to whether or not a God-thing "exists" has quite lost any sort of genuine urgency. That ghost has been so laid to rest that it is now only "the last fading smile of a cosmic Cheshire Cat."[11]

After Feuerbach and Nietzsche and Freud and Wittgenstein, not only is the divine *pantokrator* felt to be an unmanageable piece of metaphysical lumber which is without any "cash value" in the human life-world; it has also been considered by many sensitive thinkers of our age to be a morally intolerable conception which invites an attitude of reverence before a frigid monstrosity. The particular defect in classical theism which is here in view is one which has not gone unnoticed by recent philosophical theology itself. In American discussion, that highly original thinker Charles Hartshorne[12] and, more

11. Julian Huxley, *Religion without Revelation* (London: Max Parrish, 1957), p. 58.
12. See Charles Hartshorne, *Man's Vision of God and the Logic of Theism* (Chicago: Willett, Clark and Co., 1941). See also his *The Divine Relativity: A Social Conception of God* (New Haven: Yale University Press, 1948) and *Reality as Social Process* (Glencoe, Ill.: The Free Press, 1953).

recently, his brilliant interpreter, Schubert Ogden,[13] have both remarked the kind of profound offense to the dignity of man which is implicit in that worship of sheer causality which has traditionally been a part of the metaphysics of theism, of what Professor Hartshorne calls its "ontolatry."[14] That is to say, however much the God of theism has been declared to be immanent in the world of His creation, the tradition appears to have been persistently unable to explicate this immanence in a truly cogent and persuasive way. For, if the God of supernaturalism is indeed "the ground of confidence in the ultimate worth or significance of our life in the world," then He "must be conceived as a reality which is genuinely related to our life in the world and to which, therefore, both we ourselves and our various actions all make a difference as to its actual being."[15] But traditional theism has regularly conceived the reality of God to be "a reality which is in every respect absolute and whose only relations to the world are the purely nominal or external relations of the world to him."[16]

In thus failing to establish the relation between God and the world of His creatures as something genuinely reciprocal, the *philosophia perennis* has presented to the moral imagination a proposal which must seem profoundly repugnant to any man who wants to affirm the radical dignity of human life. For what we are offered is the conception of a supreme Being Who, being eternally immutable and impassive, is forever unaffected by and consequently indifferent to all the endeavors and vicissitudes which make up the human story. For such a God man's earthly pilgrimage is, ultimately, of no account, since nothing that we do or fail to do can augment or detract from the static perfection that this God enjoys. So, when we

13. See Schubert M. Ogden, *The Reality of God* (New York: Harper and Row, 1966).

14. See Professor Hartshorne's introductory essay in *Philosophers Speak of God*, ed. Charles Hartshorne and William L. Reese (Chicago: University of Chicago Press, 1953).

15. Ogden, *Reality of God*, p. 47.

16. Ibid., p. 48.

find ourselves afflicted by the distresses which flesh is heir to, we shall find no peace or consolation in Him, for "he is . . . the eternal bystander whose back is turned to the woe of the world."[17] And thus it is no wonder that, "after Auschwitz," the gifted young Jewish theologian Richard Rubenstein finds it necessary to conclude that "we live in the time of the death of God."[18]

But if there is no resurrecting that hypothesis which the Marquis de Laplace relegated to the discard at the beginning of the nineteenth century, and if supernaturalist theism can no longer be found to have any warrant in human experience —if, indeed, it is a conception which by many today is felt even to be morally intolerable—how, then, is it possible now to express the conviction that that which holds the world together and "assembles" it into a stable unity is something truly gracious? Here, most assuredly, is the real issue with which we are left *post mortem dei*. For men breathing the atmosphere of the modern world the theistic hypothesis, let us quickly grant, may be an utterly superfluous piece of intellectual baggage, insofar as it posits the "existence" of some impalpable entity standing over against and yet somehow being also pervasive throughout the space-time universe. This is what Bonhoeffer called the God of the "stop-gap,"[19] Who is brought forward as a cosmological principle wherewith the incoherences of nature and history may be theoretically resolved. But this, as Rudolf Bultmann would say, is to think "mythologically," whereas the whole emphasis of modern science commits the people of our age to the supposition that the events of nature and history are understandable only in terms of factors immanent in the events themselves.

Yet, even if we can no longer conceive the universe to have a second storey, some "realm of the divine over and above or

17. Ibid., p. 51.
18. Richard L. Rubenstein, *After Auschwitz: Radical Theology and Contemporary Judaism* (Indianapolis: Bobbs-Merrill, 1966), p. 244.
19. Bonhoeffer, *Letters and Papers from Prison*, pp. 103–04.

behind the processes of nature and history which perforates this world or breaks it by supranatural intervention"[20]—even if what Leslie Dewart calls "absolute theism"[21] is no longer an available possibility for systematic thought—the exigencies of life continue to enforce upon men the distinctively *religious* question, namely, whether or not our world is sufficiently supportive of the human enterprise to justify our conceiving it to be a truly sacramental reality, an outward expression of an inward grace. This, indeed, is the real substance of the question that, traditionally, has taken the form of the question of God; and the great challenge which is now presented to contemporary reflection is that of finding some new system of ideas whereby this profoundest concern of the human spirit can be articulated in ways that do not violate the established grammar of modern intelligence. Which is to say that our task is what Dietrich Bonhoeffer declared it to be, that of learning how to speak "in secular fashion of God," of finding a nonreligious way"[22] of exploring man's ultimate concern.

It may well be, however, that the appropriate idiom to be employed here is not one that requires to be wholly invented *ab ovo*. For, in the line of speculation reaching from Ruysbroeck through Angelus Silesius to Paul Tillich and from Eckhart and Boehme to Nicolas Berdyaev, we may discern the course of a great tradition which has steadily resisted the tendency of the *philosophia perennis* to conceive what is ultimate in reality as *a* Being above and among other beings, or as *a* Person. This is not, of course, a line of thought which derogates the conception of reality as ultimately personal, as ultimately possessing the same kind of steadiness belonging to personal relationships characterized by mutuality of trust and love. Yet it is a tradition which distrusts the anthropomorphic image as a vehicle for the expression of the personalist

20. John A. T. Robinson, *Exploration into God* (Stanford: Stanford University Press, 1967), p. 80.

21. See Leslie Dewart, *The Future of Belief* (New York: Herder and Herder, 1966), pp. 64–69.

22. Dietrich Bonhoeffer, *Letters and Papers from Prison*, pp. 92, 124.

vision, because such an image is felt to be a misleading and simplistic reduction of the mysterious immensity of what Teilhard de Chardin calls the *milieu divin*. Indeed, it is precisely this fear of all anthropomorphic representations of the Transcendent which has recurrently led the religious imagination to embrace some sort of *via negationis;* and in Eckhart, Ruysbroeck, and Boehme we get classic statements of an enduring conviction that the only adequate approach to the Divine Dark is by way of the disclamations of negative theology.

In those traditions of mystical and philosophical theology which have resisted the anthropomorphic fallacy, the controlling motive, however, has not been that of any sort of aposiopesis. The basic intention, rather, has been that of affirming the coinherence in the world of the human creature of that ecompassing reality which meets us in the terms of grace and demand and which, precisely because it is (as Eckhart said) the *Is-ness* of everything that exists, is inexpressible in the imagery of anthropomorphism. What is witnessed to is not a supernatural Person but "the dearest freshness deep down things"[23] that flows out toward the farthest peripheries of the universe and invades the most intimate neighborhood of our experience. The "Beyond" (in Bonhoeffer's familiar formulation) is found "in the midst of our life";[24] in Teilhard's phrasing, it is found to be the "within" of all things which is "coextensive with their without," "shining forth from the depths of every event, every element."[25] The world is seen to be charged with a grandeur which flames out, as Hopkins said, "like shining from shook foil," and it is beheld as gathered "to a greatness, like the ooze of oil / Crushed."[26]

This is, of course, a kind of vision—of the "all in all," of

23. Gerard Manley Hopkins, "God's Grandeur," *Poems of Gerard Manley Hopkins*, ed. Robert Bridges, 2d ed. (New York: Oxford University Press, 1938), p. 26.

24. Bonhoeffer, *Letters and Papers from Prison*, p. 93.

25. Teilhard de Chardin, *Hymn of the Universe*, trans. Simon Bartholomew (New York: Harper and Row, 1965), pp. 83, 28.

26. Gerard Manley Hopkins, "God's Grandeur."

the Divine as "nearer to us than we are to ourselves"—which is calculated to make traditional theists immediately nervous; and the charge that is quickly pronounced, almost as an automatic reflex, is that so to dispel all duality between the world and the Divine is to embrace a monism which is essentially pantheistic. And, indeed, it is a method of thought which is close enough to pantheism for a pantheistic echo to be heard in its proper name, which is *panentheism*. Now, to be sure, a fully developed panentheism declares that there is nothing "outside" the Divine, that it has no opposite—since, if anything were "outside" it, it would be hedged about by some limitation and would not be divine. God, as the anonymous author of *The Cloud of Unknowing* puts it, "is the being of all." But to maintain that the Divine is in everything and that everything is in the Divine is by no means to assert, as pantheism does, that the world and God are coterminous and that the multiplicity of finite existence is wholly absorbed in some impersonal Absolute.

If "the creature is one with God in the very act of being other than God"[27] and if diversity and distinction are, therefore, included within the unity of the Divine, then the very nerve of pantheism is broken, because it conceives the particularities of finite existence to be illusory, since they are ultimately swallowed up into the unity of God and finally nullified. But panentheism says that the multiplicity of finite existence and the unity of the Divine are not ultimately discontinuous. So it does not assert that the unity of God nullifies the individuality and diversity that belong to the world of creatures, for if they, in their distinctness from God, were not truly real, then God Himself "would not be free to include *real* diversity in his unity."[28] Nor is the panentheist prepared to say (as the pantheist tends in effect to do) that "God minus the universe equals nothing."[29] Indeed, he conceives the Di-

27. Alan W. Watts, *Behold the Spirit: A Study in the Necessity of Mystical Religion* (New York: Pantheon Books, 1947), p. 145.
28. Ibid., p. 146.
29. Ibid., p. 148.

vine to be *totaliter aliter;* and "God's 'othering' of himself," far from being considered an illusion, is understood as "the free gift of his Being to creatures who otherwise might not have existed."[30] Which is to say that for Eckhart as for Berdyaev, for Boehme as for Tillich, for Johannes Tauler as for Charles Hartshorne, the frontier between the world and God is an "open frontier."[31]

The method of thought which is here being spoken of as panentheism has, of course, been so variously expressed in Western philosophy and theology that it can hardly be conceived as constituting a unitary tradition. For it can be discerned as an important tendency in thinkers as divergent from one another as Augustine, the medieval Franciscans (Alexander of Hales, Bonaventura, and Matthew of Aquasparta), the great mystics of the fourteenth century (Eckhart, Tauler, Heinrich Suso, Ruysbroeck, Mother Julian), the German Idealists, and such men of this century as Whitehead and Berdyaev and Tillich. But though it would appear to have been an impulse that has splayed out in many diverse directions, its persistence through the centuries is to be remarked in the continually recurrent effort to conceive the world as a sacramental reality, not by reason of some hidden relation that it bears to *a* supernatural Being (the *ens realissimum* or the *ens singularissimum*), but, rather, by reason of its being indwelt by *esse ipsum.* And thus it would seem that, if the sacramental vision is again to be set forth—in terms that are assimilable by modern mentality—it is to this line of thought that recourse should be taken.

Now it is just as we begin to search out the possibility of articulating a sacramental vision of reality which is not dependent on what John Robinson calls "the supranaturalist projection"[32] (of *a* transcendent Being or Person)—it is just at this point that we ought to be put in mind of that massive

30. Ibid., p. 145.
31. Robinson, *Exploration into God,* p. 82.
32. See Ibid., pp. 28–32.

structure of thought which Martin Heidegger, the last great genius of philosophy in our period, has been developing over nearly fifty years. For it is by way of the kind of inquiry Heidegger has launched that we have newly available today a brilliantly original development of that minority tradition in Western religious and philosophical thought which has resisted the supranaturalist projections of the *philosophia perennis.* And it may well be that the profound meditation on the subject of Being which has constituted the principal effort of this magisterial German teacher points toward the direction that any restatement of the sacramental idea needs to take, if it is to be genuinely appropriable by modern sensibility.

To such a proposal there are, of course, those who will doubtless want immediately to raise the objection that nothing is less likely to appeal to modern sensibility than inquiries into the nature of Being, since (as it will be argued) the very notion of Being posits something whose existence cannot, in the nature of the case, be established by those procedures of verification which are decisive for our predominantly empiricist mentality. And certainly it has been the testimony of the reigning school of contemporary philosophy that the concept of Being affords an instance of nothing more substantial than "the way in which a consideration of grammar leads to metaphysics." That is to say, we are afflicted by "the superstition . . . that, to every word or phrase that can be the grammatical subject of a sentence, there must somewhere be a real entity corresponding."[33] We have the noun *being* in our inherited language, and thus we mistakenly suppose that there is some discriminable entity to which the word refers—but, as recent analytic philosophy reminds us, in point of hard fact no such entity exists. And at the point at which, with a great flourish, this lesson is laid down by A. J. Ayer in his famous book, *Language, Truth and Logic,* his way of alluding to Heidegger makes it clear that he regards such arguments as he brings for-

33. A. J. Ayer, *Language, Truth and Logic,* rev. ed. (London: Victor Gollancz, 1946), pp. 42–43.

ward here to be an effective broom with which the mind may be swept clean of the heavy confusions which derive from this German metaphysician.

In this connection, however, it needs to be said in Heidegger's defense that, unlike many of his Anglo-American contemporaries, it has never occurred to him to suppose that Being belongs to the category of "things." Indeed, he has often been at pains to remind us that Being is quite radically misconceived if it is thought of as any sort of "object" (*Gegenstand*) standing over against the human "subject"; and in the "Letter on Humanism" ("Über den 'Humanismus'") of 1947 he declares quite explicitly that "Being is wider than every particular being and is yet closer to man than every being, whether it be a rock, an animal, a work of art, a machine, an angel. . . ."[34] Which is to say that we do not confront Being as we confront a table or a tree, for it is that which is constantly present in all the things of this world, enabling them to be whatever it is for which they are destined by their inner constitution.

Yet so to speak of Being is not to assign it the status of a universal attribute belonging to every particular being, for Kant's lesson of long ago (in book 2 of *The Critique of Pure Reason*) is not to be forgotten—that unlike the predication of redness or roundness about a thing, we do not in any way increase what is known about it when we simply declare that it exists. To say that a thing *is*, is not to have specified one of its distinguishing properties; and thus, since being is not a stipulable property of things, the logic of classes forbids its being conceived as constituting any sort of genus. For, obviously, since the notion of being implies no distinction among already existing things, it would simply be tautologous to regard it as designating the only kind of class which it might reasonably be considered to denote, namely, all things which do exist.

The inevitable negativity in what must initially be one's approach to the concept of Being need not be taken, however,

34. Martin Heidegger, "Über den 'Humanismus,'" in *Platons Lehre von der Wahrheit* (Bern: A. Francke, 1947), p. 76.

as confirming the essential emptiness which is imputed to the concept by philosophic skepticism. And it is a part of Heidegger's distinction to have shown that conceiving of Being as an entity or substance or attribute or class does not by any means exhaust the conceptual possibilities. His method of discourse makes it clear that Being is for him what the language of traditional philosophy calls a transcendental—namely, a reality which is to be reached only, as it were, by moving through the contingent realities of nature and history and which is therefore "above" the ordinary categories of reflection. But his great book of 1927, *Being and Time* (*Sein und Zeit*), makes it equally clear that Heidegger does not regard the path to Being as one which proceeds from the indigence of finitude toward a rational demonstration—by way of inference and the principle of causality—of something like the Absolute of Idealist philosophy.

Indeed, it might be said that, for Heidegger, Being is to be approached not at all theoretically but existentially, for Being is not that which man stands out from or over against. On the contrary, it is that in which he most deeply participates, that by which he is most deeply grasped. Thus the cognitive relation in which he stands with respect to Being is, as we are reminded in the opening pages of *Being and Time*, an affair of a "hermeneutical circle"—which is to say that the interpreter is already a part of that which is to be interpreted, so that the process of interpretation must involve a circular reasoning, since, in the nature of the case, the interpreter begins his task with some inward grasp of that which awaits elucidation. So, instead of involving some theoretical process of deduction, the intellectual act whereby one takes hold of the nature of Being involves a descent into the depths of one's own humanity. The cognitive effort entails, in other words, not a "transcendental analytic" but an "existential analytic," and it is this to which the book of 1927 is very largely given over.

Here, in *Being and Time*, it is *Dasein* which is one of the decisive terms of Heidegger's argument. This Germanism—

which means literally *being-there* and is not customarily translated in non-German discussions of Heidegger's philosophy—is Heidegger's technical term for the human mode of being: he considers man's distinctive passion to be so much one for interrogating the nature of his existence that he deserves, indeed, simply to be regarded himself as *Dasein.* "*Dasein,*" as Heidegger says, "is an entity for which, in its Being, that Being is an issue."[35] And since it is in the human quest for Being that we have our most immediate access to Being, it is the exploration of *Dasein* to which the book of 1927 is largely devoted. For Heidegger's most basic supposition in this period of his career appears to have been that the path to Being is one that leads through an analysis of those structures of existence belonging to the particular being whose nature requires him to raise the question of Being. It was, in short, the study of *Dasein* which he regarded as constituting what he called "fundamental ontology," and the profoundly original and exciting inquiry that was carried forward in this vein—into the nature of anxiety (*Angst*), care (*Sorge*), transcendence (*Transzendenz*), temporality (*Zeitlichkeit*), the experience of death, and the meaning of authenticity (*Eigentlichkeit*)—makes *Being and Time* one of the great classic monuments in the literature of modern existentialism.

Almost immediately after the appearance of this book, however, it would seem that Heidegger's thought underwent a certain reversal (*Kehre*), and this "turning" is to be detected already in the inaugural lecture ("What is Metaphysics?")[36] which he delivered in 1929 on succeeding Edmund Husserl in the chair of philosophy at the University of Freiburg. Here, as

35. Martin Heidegger, *Being and Time*, trans. John Macquarrie and Edward Robinson (New York: Harper and Row, 1962), p. 236.
36. Martin Heidegger, *Was ist Metaphysik?* 5th ed. (Frankfurt-am-Main: Vittorio Klostermann, 1949). An English version of the lecture, ("What Is Metaphysics?" trans. R. F. C. Hull and Alan Crick), together with the "Postscript" which Heidegger prepared in 1943, appears in *Existence and Being*, ed. Werner Brock (Chicago: Henry Regnery Co., 1949), pp. 355–92.

he confronted Freiburg colleagues representing the various faculties and sciences making up the university, Heidegger chose to attack the most difficult question with which a philosopher might wrestle before such an audience—namely, the question as to whether there is anything at all remaining for the philosopher to do, after the practitioners of the several scientific disciplines have begun their diverse labors. With a strange kind of bravado, he proceeded in effect quickly to grant that, indeed, once the established sciences have launched all their various inquiries into the nature of the existing world, "nothing" is left over. But, then, in a brilliant tour de force, he declared that very nothingness to be the ultimate subject of philosophy.

The lecture makes it clear, however, that this nothingness which is to be addressed by metaphysical philosophy is no mere logical conundrum but, rather, an existential datum of the most concrete sort. For man (as it had been argued in *Being and Time*) is a creature who finds his life encircled by darkness: the human adventure begins by our being "thrown" into a world which is not of our making, and the transiency of our life looks only toward the final certitude of death. Man, therefore, is an anxious creature because he is aware of the radical finitude of his existence. The experience of anxiety may, to be sure, be felt only intermittently and at rare intervals, since we are normally caught up in all those inconsequential routines of daily life that tend to obscure what is fundamentally hazardous in our condition. But, when we are stung by that terrible dread to which we are ultimately fated, then, immediately —as we feel ourselves to be moving merely from "thrownness" (*Geworfenheit*) to death—the world sinks into a profound kind of insignificance, and the only thing that remains is the primordial Nothingness.

Yet, as Heidegger argues in the Freiburg lecture, it is precisely the unhinging encounter with Nothing that enlivens the mind's awareness of our being compassed round about by something more than mere Nothingness, namely, the multiplicity of actual beings that make up our world-environment. "Only because Nothing is revealed in the very basis of our *Dasein*," he says, "is it possible for the utter strangeness of what-is to dawn on us."[37] It is, in other words, the threatening specter of Nothing which awakens in us that ontological shock wherewith we notice that, indeed, we face not Nothing but *something*. Thus, Heidegger suggests, the old proposition *ex nihilo nihil fit* ought perhaps to be made to say *ex nihilo omne ens qua ens fit*.

Now it may, of course, at first appear that the Freiburg lecture is espousing the purest sort of nihilism; but, as Heidegger makes plain in the "Postscript" of 1943, the metaphysic of Nothingness was intended only to be a propaedeutic looking forward to a metaphysic of Being. His "Postscript" wants, in effect, to say that if in that lecture he seemed to be equating Being with Nothing, this was done only in the manner of a conceit—but a conceit, as he would insist, which is not itself essentially illicit. For, like "Nothing," Being itself is not *a* being; and since it is a non-entity, it is, like "Nothing," *absolutely* different from all beings. As a consequence, it cannot be fitted into any of the categories of existence. It is, in short, a "transcendental" which we begin to approach when the question is asked, "Why is there anything at all, rather than nothing?"

Just two years after the appearance of *Being and Time* Heidegger was, in other words, already committing himself to what has come to be the great quest of his career and one of the great quests of modern intellectual life. For he was now a man in pursuit of the last objective which beckons the philosophical imagination and which is none other than Being itself. But though by the early 1930's his principal concern was no longer the kind of analysis of the human condition which he had undertaken in *Being and Time*, the tendency of many recent interpreters to emphasize very sharply this "turning" in his development ought now perhaps to be somewhat cur-

37. Heidegger, "What Is Metaphysics?" p. 378.

tailed. For, even in the earlier phase of his career, the study of
Dasein was conceived primarily to be a way of proceeding to
the question of Being; and though his early work has a notably existentialist slant which is, to be sure, distinguishable
from the predominantly ontological emphasis of his later writing, he is himself by no means unjustified in his insistence
that, early and late, it is indeed the question of Being which
has been the overriding concern of his thought for nearly fifty
years. Above all else, it is for this, he contends, that he has
sought a new hearing.[38]

Over these past decades, however, Heidegger has gone
about his elected task with an abiding sense of facing into
enormously resistant head winds. For, as he frequently reminds us, we in the modern West are a people so committed
to the superstitions of positivism that we have virtually lost
any capacity for performing an act of true attention before the
sheer ontological weight and depth of the world. The term
positivism is not, to be sure, a part of Heidegger's lexicon: he
speaks, rather, of our great penchant for "calculative thinking" (*rechnendes Denken*).[39] But the calculative approach to
the world is of the very essence of the positivist's intention
to deal with reality solely in the terms of mastery and control
and manipulation; and, in Heidegger's sense of our situation,
it is precisely this essentially predatory motive that constitutes
the sovereign passion dominating the mentality of our period.
It is a passion to arrange and organize, to regulate, and to turn
things to practical account, and its underlying assumption is
that reality is wholly coextensive with the world of public operables, with the things that can be weighed and measured
and manipulated.

38. See Martin Heidegger, "Preface" to William J. Richardson, S.J.,
Heidegger: Through Phenomenology to Thought (The Hague: Martinus
Nijhoff, 1963), pp. viii–xxiii.

39. See Martin Heidegger, *Gelassenheit* (Pfullingen: Gunther Neske
Verlag, 1959); the English version, trans. John M. Anderson and E. Hans
Freund, bears the title *Discourse on Thinking* (New York: Harper and
Row, 1966).

Now, however much man's conduct of his affairs may on certain levels require the instrumentalist orientation of calculative thinking, it deserves to be recognized as involving a highly specialized sort of hermeneutic which may enable us to control our external environment with great sophistication but which does, nevertheless, exact a great cost, in the degree to which it tends to shut us up in that cruelest of jails which is established by the limits of commonsense rationality. And it is Heidegger's contention that, until this jail is broken out of, we do not give ourselves any chance to hear the call of Being. For when the things of earth are approached in that grasping, manipulative spirit of the calculative reason and when our sole intention is to make them obedient to some enterprise of science or engineering—when they are simply considered to be material for one or another kind of observation and experiment and use—then they become inert and fall silent.

Indeed, in such an advanced technological culture as our own, this "silence" of Being is to be alleviated only by what is perhaps the most extraordinary feat of imagination that technological man can perform, of managing for a time to shut down all the well-driven machines of his science and his engineering. For it is only when the world begins no longer to be approached merely as something to be "attacked"[40] in the manner of a technological project—it is only when we consent to approach it in the spirit of what Heidegger calls *Gelassenheit* (that is, surrender, abandonment, acquiescence)—it is only then that the "voice" of Being begins to be heard. What is required is a throttling of our great consuming passion to invade every nook and cranny of the world with our concepts and categories and schemes of manipulation. For, until we have learned again the discipline of "letting-be,"[41] we shall not achieve that condition of what Heidegger calls "releasement

40. Heidegger, *Discourse on Thinking*, p. 88.
41. See Martin Heidegger, "On the Essence of Truth," in *Existence and Being*, pp. 319–51.

toward things"[42] which is nothing other than an attitude of simple enthrallment before the sheer concreteness and specificity of all the various givens of the earth.

This is, however, an attitude, a way of *receiving* the world, that rests on quite a different sort of rationality from that which customarily prevails in our culture. For the mind does not become alive to what is most primitively marvelous in the affairs of life until it subordinates calculative thinking to what Heidegger speaks of as "meditative thinking"—by which, as he says, he means utter "openness" to radical mystery, to the mystery of there being *something* rather than nothing.[43] Meditative thinking is a thinking in which the originating force proceeds, as it were, not so much from the mind itself as from that under which it stands, so that we feel a claim being laid upon us, a demand being levied against us. The meditative thinker knows himself to be addressed by something transcendent, by something wholly other than himself; and he is not so much acting on as he is being acted upon, so that the knowledge which is brought to him as a result of his "meditation" is something like a gift. Yet he is by no means wholly inactive, for taking up an attitude of meditative openness to the world means "paying heed" to the strange kind of stoutness by which its things and creatures are steadied and supported. And it is by this most exacting labor of imagination that at last we are brought into the neighborhood of Being.

But what is Being? In his writings of the last thirty-five years, it is this ultimate question which Heidegger may often seem to be evading as constantly as he is raising it, for again and again it slides into view and then quickly slips lizardlike away, leaving only its tail in our hands. On one point, to be sure, he is quite emphatic, that "Being is not God."[44] For the God of traditional metaphysics, or of what he calls "onto-theo-logy," is *an* entity or object, a particular being, albeit the

---

42. Heidegger, *Discourse on Thinking*, pp. 54–55.
43. Ibid., pp. 46–57.
44. Heidegger, "Über den 'Humanismus,' " p. 76.

Highest or the Supreme being—but Being itself is not *a* being,
not even the totality of all beings. Indeed, when thought of in
relation to the world of particular beings, it must be considered to be "that-which-is not," or Nothing. Yet (as he says in
the "Postscript" to "What is Metaphysics?") this Nothing
"is not a nugatory Nothing," since its vastness is precisely
"that which gives every being the warrant to be."[45] Thus it is
nothing less than Being itself.

Nor are Heidegger's negatives in regard to Being confined to
the issue of its definability in theistic terms, though these negatives become somewhat less absolute when he begins to ex-
amine Being in relation to those modalities which would, for-
mally, appear to be quite distinct from it. In his *Introduction
to Metaphysics* (*Einführung in die Metaphysik*),[46] for example,
he considers Being in relation to becoming and in relation to
appearance (that which "seems-to-be"). And though he wants
finally to say that Being is neither becoming nor appearance,
his negative is a qualified negative. For since becoming is a
process whereby something more fully develops into itself,
that which becomes does in some sense already exist; and,
therefore, becoming cannot be considered as absolutely anti-
thetical to Being. Yet Being, though it includes within itself a
dynamic element, is not mere process, mere permutation, mere
becoming. Similarly, that which "seems-to-be" could not in
any way at all submit itself to our inspection if it did not in
some sense truly exist; and furthermore, since Being is a transcendental, it must always be approached mediately, by way of
the particular phenomena that make up the world of appearance. Yet, though Being is always given in, with, and through
its appearances, it is not itself simply appearance, since it is
that which enables things, as it were, to be gathered together
and to stand before us: so it must in some sense be concealed.

45. Heidegger, "Postscript" to "What Is Metaphysics?" p. 385.
46. See Martin Heidegger, *Einführung in die Metaphysik* (Tübingen:
Max Niemeyer Verlag, 1953); the English version, trans. Ralph Manheim, bears the title *An Introduction to Metaphysics* (New Haven: Yale
University Press, 1959).

Now these are but the merest handful of the negatives with which the Heideggerian literature is strewn on the question of Being, and they convey something of the extreme reticence which Heidegger very carefully keeps about man's most primal encounter with reality. Yet his final intention is not that of invoking any *via negationis*, for he conceives Being to have a veritable "mission" to the world of earth, and to this he wants to give as positive an utterance as our human language will permit.

Already in his book of 1929 on Kant[47] Heidegger was beginning to speak of the foundation of ontological inquiry as that "pure horizon" of intelligibility "in which the Being of beings becomes antecedently discernible." And it is such a nonobjectifying idiom that he has consistently employed in his writings of more recent years—in, for example, the "Letter on Humanism"; the essays on Hölderlin;[48] the *Introduction to Metaphysics;* the book of 1954, *What Evokes Thought? (Was heisst Denken?)*; and the two books of 1957, *The Principle of Ground (Der Satz vom Grund)* and *Identity and Difference (Identität und Differenz).*[49]

The testimony being made in these and numerous other works seems calculated to suggest that it is the mission of Being to establish the possibility of *presence* for all particular beings. Being is that primal energy which gathers things into themselves and so keeps them thus assembled that they can stand out before the gaze of intelligence. *A* being might be said to be simply that-which-is-present, that-which-is-in-the-open; whereas Being itself *is* that Openness which lights up

47. Martin Heidegger, *Kant und das Problem der Metaphysik* (Bonn: Cohen, 1929; 2nd ed., Frankfurt-am-Main: Vittorio Klostermann, 1951). An English version, trans. J. S. Churchill, bears the title *Kant and the Problem of Metaphysics* (Bloomington: Indiana University Press, 1962).

48. Martin Heidegger, *Erläuterungen zu Hölderlins Dichtung* (Frankfurt-am-Main: Vittorio Klostermann, 1944).

49. Martin Heidegger, *Identität und Differenz* (Pfullingen: Günther Neske, 1957). An English version, trans. Kurt F. Leidecker, bears the title *Essays in Metaphysics: Identity and Difference* (New York: Philosophical Library, 1960).

the things of earth, which enables us to behold them in their radical actuality, and which is never itself, therefore, conceivable as a being. One suspects that Heidegger would be inclined to say that the very question "What is Being?" expresses the profoundest misconception that the mind can entertain, for its presupposition is that Being is, indeed, objectively definable. But, as one of his interpreters reminds us, "Being is beyond all 'whats' and 'whiches,' all separations and distinctions."[50] One cannot point to it as one points to a table or a gazelle, for it is itself precisely that which makes it possible for all objects to have objectivity. And, inevitably, that by which all things are lighted up and shown forth must, in its own absolute interiority, remain hidden.

Yet, though Being is hidden and far away because it is the source (*Ursprung*) of all reality, it nevertheless—as Heidegger likes to say—"hails" us, and this hailing consists precisely in the generosity with which it permits the things of earth to "come-to-presence."[51] Their presence, in other words, *is* the hail, the salutation, which Being addresses to us; and since they are present only because Being has imparted itself to them in the manner of a gift, any truly meditative thinking must, in effect, be an act of thanksgiving. For thinking of the most fundamental kind involves our "hailing" Being, which is to say that we respond to its primary hail by receiving and accepting the plenitude which it bestows upon us. And since we know this plenitude to be not of our own creation, since we recognize it to be in no way a part of ourselves, since it is the sheer otherness of Being itself and of its self-giving, genuinely meditative thinking becomes, inevitably, an affair of thanksgiving for the incalculable munificence with which Being lets things be.

Indeed, it is just at this point that we have at last before us the terms which Heidegger doubtless prefers above all others

50. Marjorie Grene, *Martin Heidegger* (London: Bowes & Bowes, 1957), p. 111.
51. See Heidegger, *Erläuterungen zu Hölderlins Dichtung*, passim.

when Being is to be spoken of. For the formula which seems more adequate to his vision than any other is that which is suggested by the phrase "letting-be" (*Seinlassen*), and this, in the final analysis, is what he conceives to be the mission and the very essence of Being—"the letting-be of beings" (*das Seinlassen von Seiendem*). Here, he would say, is the ultimate mystery of Being, and the mystery which it is the peculiar privilege of man to contemplate, that Being does not hoard up its plenitude within itself (as, conceivably, it might) but rather, with an infinite liberality, takes as its mission the bestowal of itself upon the world of time and finitude and contingency. Being "gives" itself to the world of beings; and it is this primordial dispensation, Heidegger believes, which constitutes the alpha and omega of any truly meditative thought.

Now the whole vision of things which this great German thinker has been developing over more than forty years does, of course, quite manifestly move toward a profoundly religious outlook. Yet Heidegger has regularly declared, in book after book, that the conception of Being is not translatable into the "God" of classical theism; for, like Paul Tillich, he regards traditional theism as having meant by God *a* being Who, even when conceived as the *ens realissimum*, was, nevertheless, one being among other beings and therefore less ultimate than Being itself. As we are reminded, however, by one of Heidegger's most distinguished interpreters, John Macquarrie, the question of God's "existence" is, most essentially, not the question as to "whether some entity or other exists, but [rather, the question as to] whether Being has such a character as would fulfill man's quest for grace."[52] To affirm God's "existence," in other words, is not to assert that a particular being —the Supreme Being—dwells in some invisible realm behind or beyond the phenomenal world. It is, rather, to declare, as a matter of radical faith, that Being is steadfast, reliable, gracious, and deserves our trust. To say that God "exists" is, in

52. John Macquarrie, *Studies in Christian Existentialism* (Philadelphia: Westminster Press, 1965), p. 12.

having also considered (in the present chapter) how the sacramental idea itself may be reconceived independently of supernaturalist theism, it may not be inappropriate to complete the design of this little book by turning, finally, to a major poet of our generation for a particular example of the sacramental imagination at work on the living body of the world. Since the sacramental principle is here being envisaged as a possibility of "secular" faith, it seems tactically wise not to have recourse to such poets as Eliot and Auden and Edwin Muir and David Jones, whose sacramental idiom is heavily dependent on the great traditions of Christian belief. Outside this circle, however, there are numerous figures any one of whom might be fitted into our pattern—William Carlos Williams, St.-John Perse, René Char perhaps, Marianne Moore, Richard Eberhart, Dylan Thomas, and many others. And, among these, it is in the work of Theodore Roethke's last years that there is to be found a particularly rich instance of poetic "sacramentation": so it is to his legacy that the concluding chapter is devoted. The choice of Roethke in this connection, though, is not at all prompted by any supposition that his poetry is directly associable with the philosophy of Heidegger. Indeed, though his interests covered a large range of systematic thought, he very probably never actually read the Heideggerian texts; and his placement in the context of these reflections is made possible, therefore, only by reason of the high congruence between the essential shape and thrust of his vision and that general pattern of which Heidegger has been taken to be the great exemplar in recent philosophic tradition.

Chapter Three THE

EXAMPLE

OF ROETHKE

In his brilliant and seminal book of 1954 on the nature of symbolic language, *The Burning Fountain*, the late Philip Wheelwright proposes that there are four basic ways whereby the imagination may be considered, in one or another of its phases, to reckon with the world's multifarious reality. It may, he suggests, choose simply to contemplate, in an attitude of the strictest attention, the various particulars which experience brings its way, seeking with great intensity to grasp these particulars in their radical individuality. This, as he says, is the way taken by the "Confrontative Imagination," and it leads toward such a pure concentration upon what is unique in the given reality that the self finds that reality "confronting it as a *thou* and becomes in turn a *thou* before the presence of its object."[1] But quite a different approach may be taken: instead of igniting the object with the kind of mesmerizing power by which it is endowed when responded to in the dimension of the simplicity of its sheer presence, the imagination may choose to act "upon its object by stylizing and distancing it."[2] This is the way of the "Stylistic Imagination," whose principal effort involves "a kind of distancing ... which

1. Philip Wheelwright, *The Burning Fountain: A Study in the Language of Symbolism* (Bloomington: Indiana University Press, 1954), p. 81.
2. Ibid., p. 78.

consists of 'putting the phenomenon, so to speak, out of gear with our practical, actual self' and thereby looking at it with a fresh objectivity."[3] When, however, the concrete reality or event (*Phänomen*) is perceived as an "Eminent Instance" of some primordial or generic reality (*Urphänomen*), the way being taken, says Wheelwright, is that of "the Archetypal Imagination, which sees the particular object as embodying and adumbrating suggestions of universality."[4] Here the self is given over to an impression of what is paradigmatic in the specific things and happenings of life, and they are appropriated in terms of "the perduring archetypes which they express and symbolize."[5] But, of course, the fusion which the mind performs may not be so much between the concrete and the general as between two or more concrete units of experience. This, in Wheelwright's scheme, represents the fourth great mode of imaginative perception, the way of the "Metaphoric Imagination," which involves the mind's unification of a given multiplicity into an organic whole, but with a kind of tact that preserves in some significant degree the heterogeneousness of the various elements being unified.

Now, of these four types of imagining, it is perhaps the confrontative and the archetypal which most nearly define that way of receiving the world which deserves to be called sacramental. For, wherever the sacramental imagination is at work on the material of human experience, the dictates of what Heidegger calls "calculative" reason have been so hushed as to permit an attitude of simple enchantment before the irrevocability whereby the things and creatures of this world are what they are, in their utter specificity. All the particular realities making up our earthly environment are approached, in

3. *Ibid.*, p. 82. Wheelwright is quoting from Edward Bullough, " 'Psychic Distance' as a Factor in Art and an Aesthetic Principle," *British Journal of Psychology*, 5 (June 1912): 87 ff.
4. *Ibid.*, p. 78.
5. *Ibid.*, p. 88. Wheelwright is here paraphrasing Goethe.

other words, in a spirit of radical amazement (at their sheer
givenness), of acquiescence, of "letting-be"; each is so heark-
ened to that it becomes, as it were, a *thou*, the human subject
itself in turn becoming a *thou* in the presence of its object.
But then, inevitably, as the concrete particular is confronted
with such intensity, it takes on the lustre of a "something
more" and is felt to be an outward and visible expression of
something *else* which is wonderful and has value. In short, it
is conceived in some sort to be a sign or token of "numinous"
reality, of the tremendous mystery of the Holy. Thus it is that
the confrontative and archetypal modes of imagining are
joined in a sacramental apprehension of the things and events
of human life.

In the poetic universe of our period, however, it is a notably
minor part that has been played by the confrontative and
archetypal modes of the imagination. For they are its more
passive forms; the stylistic and metaphoric modes entail a
very much more active kind of handling of the world. And in
a time when the continuing validity and effectiveness of the
great received traditions of faith have been widely felt to be
problematic, at the very least, it was no doubt to be expected
that the modern poet should feel it necessary to expend a great
labor, either in distancing himself from the immediate dis-
order (toward the end of winning some final mastery of it) or
in trying to achieve some new fusion of the heterogeneities
of modern experience. His tendency, in other words, has been
in various ways to commit himself to the stylistic or, more
regularly even, to the metaphoric imagination.

So we do not have many large examples of "sacramentation"
in the important poetry of this century which carries our pe-
riod-style. That great dynasty presiding over the classic period
of twentieth-century modernism—Valéry, Rilke, Pound, the
early Eliot, Apollinaire—were, most of them, technicians in
the art of dismantling and reassembling the world; they were
artists as impatient with any preexistent ontological order as
with inherited social and political patterns. In Anglo-American

tradition, the Eliot of the *Quartets,* the later Yeats in his "tragic joy," the Williams of *Paterson,* and the Stevens of *The Auroras of Autumn* are exceptions, along with that most elegant "literalist of the imagination," Marianne Moore—but these are exceptions that tend only to emphasize how much the irony and wit and intellect so distinctive of the classic texts of our century's poetry are generally to be found having been at the service of some highly ambitious program for recasting or remodeling the human reality.

Nor would it seem that an essentially different purpose is to be found in the movement launched by that second or "middle" generation which entered the literary life in the period extending, say, from 1930 into the early 1940's. There is, to be sure, an angel in Richard Eberhart's verse play *Devils and Angels* who, in a visitation to one of the characters, says:

> I come to bring you harmony and serenity,
> To remind you of a height beyond your condition,
> I have come like a blinding of the insight,
> Those times you have had in the night without words,
> . . . .
> Those apparently unreal and disjointed times
> When you felt the world as an immaculate radiance
> In the hand of God; in those incredible intuitions
> I was always there, beneficent and without harm to you.[6]

And, on the American scene, this note of celebration is struck again and again in the poetry of Richard Wilbur and of Eberhart himself—and occasionally, with astonishing brilliance and poignancy, in Auden's work of the past twenty years. But, of our major poets of the "middle" generation, it is by no means the characteristic emphasis of Stanley Kunitz or John Berryman or Robert Lowell or of the late Randall Jarrell.

Of this American generation, however, there is one figure of immense distinction, the late Theodore Roethke, whose en-

6. Richard Eberhart, "Devils and Angels," *Collected Verse Plays* (Chapel Hill: University of North Carolina Press, 1962), pp. 113–14.

tire career was a search for ways of turning "the wild disordered language of the natural heart" into a song whose "broken music" might be an adequate sacrifice of praise and thanksgiving for the great things of earth. In recent poetry, he offers what is perhaps the crucial instance of a truly sacramental vision of our human inheritance.

Indeed, there is rarely to be found in the literature of our period a body of poetry so predominantly psalmic and doxological as Roethke's: almost everywhere, it seems, the poet's voice is lifted up in jubilant alleluias announcing "the soul's immediate joy" and praising the glory and greatness of the world. In the remarkable sequence of poems entitled "Four for Sir John Davies," which appeared in his book of 1953, *The Waking*,[7] he speaks of his "need [for] a place to sing," of how his very blood leaps "with a wordless song." In a poem called "The Renewal," which is included in *Words for the Wind* (1958), he says: "I teach my sighs to lengthen into songs. . . ." And his verse, even after having descended into the darkest things imaginable, wants to sound a hymnic note and to be a sort of lay canticle, for this poet (as he notes in "The Dying Man," *Words for the Wind*) is one whose

> heart sways with the world.
> I am that final thing,
> A man learning to sing.

As he says in one of the last poems ("Sequence, Sometimes Metaphysical," included in the posthumous volume of 1964, *The Far Field*), "I'll make a broken music, or I'll die."

But the resonance of song which is so constantly to be heard in Roethke's poetry is by no means the consequence of something merely willed by a resolutely gladsome spirit. For his jubilation is not only often a narrowly won achievement on the further side of despair; it is also always, finally, a response to a music which is *heard*—in the spheres and in those places

7. A bibliography of the works of Theodore Roethke, including those cited in the text, will be found at the end of this chapter.

of the world regularly inhabited by the human creature. Indeed, he finds "the earth itself a tune," whose rocks and birds and trees and living souls are all minstrels "singing into the beyond." And thus the habit Roethke's poetry has of recurrently breaking into song represents, as Heidegger would say, his way of "hailing" a world whose *presence* is itself conveyed as a kind of music. This is what lies behind his venturing, in the beautiful poem "O Lull Me, Lull Me" (*Praise to the End!* [1951]), so risky a declaration as

> I could say hello to things;
> . . . .
> I see what sings!
> What sings!

Or again, as he says with a most moving brevity and terseness in the great cycle of poems called "Meditations of an Old Woman" (*Words for the Wind*):

> In my grandmother's inner eye,
> . . . .
> A bird always kept singing.
> She was a serious woman.

In a love poem written towards the end of his life, "Light Listened" (*The Far Field*), Roethke concludes his song about one than whose "ways with a man" nothing "could be more nice" by saying, "Light listened when she sang." Which puts us in mind of the great line in the opening poem of "North American Sequence" (*The Far Field*), where the poet declares: "The light cries out, and I am there to hear. . . ." One might say that, for Roethke, the earth is a singing earth whose things and creatures answer and listen to one another in their singing, so that all their songs make up a vast universal dialogue and one great antiphonal hymn wherein the infinitely varied minstrelsy of Creation sings "into the beyond" its perpetual exultets and magnificats.

A vulgar literalism will, of course, immediately nominate

such a sense of reality animistic or panpsychist, and Roethke's vision will be conceived to represent a curiously self-indulgent primitivism. Yet this would by no means be a particularly sensitive verdict, and certainly it is not the inevitable response. Indeed, what Roethke understood (through processes of poetic intuition)—and what certain systematic philosophers are beginning to perceive—is that the myth of the world as nothing but a huge *res extensa*, silent and dead and immeasurable, is no less improbable than the crudest animism. For things which are merely things-in-themselves simply do not exist. In point of fact, any truly cognitive encounter with the world inevitably involves its being drawn into a kind of family relationship with the human spirit, since (as Conrad Bonifazi reminds us in his profound and strangely neglected book, *A Theology of Things*) things do not even begin to exhibit any sort of significant meaning or value until we identify ourselves with them in one way or another. The act of knowing, in other words, "is born and nourished in some kind of *enthusiastic* association."[8] As Edmund Husserl never tired of saying, "What things are . . . they are as things of experience"[9] —by which he meant that, though they exist in their own right, they can be known only as they are experienced, and to be experienced they must be drawn into dynamic interrelationship with human consciousness.

But, as Husserl was also at pains to tell modern philosophy, human experience does not move wholly within the dimensions of the fact-world which is spread out before us in space and time. We take this world for granted, of course, and it is one of the great limiting boundaries of the human enterprise; but sensory perception—which, in its most highly disciplined forms, is our way of grasping the fact-world—is not at all our only means of access to reality, and the world

8. Conrad Bonifazi, *A Theology of Things* (Philadelphia: J. B. Lippincott Co., 1967), p. 165.

9. Edmund Husserl, *Ideas*, trans. W. R. Boyce Gibson (New York: Macmillan Co., 1931), p. 88.

of human consciousness embraces far more than simply the contents of sensory perception. Indeed, the insight with which Husserl inaugurated the whole program of modern phenomenology consisted very largely in his discerning that, actually, there is no such thing as "experience" until something more than a merely perceptual act occurs.

His contention, basically, is that a thing does not really enter into our selfhood, into our sense of the world and of our own existence, until we have done something more than merely glance at it. For the world which is "out there" must be "immanentized," must be not simply glanced at but attended to; and only then do we receive its meaning (through an act of radical intuition) and appropriate it as a matter of "experience," of "intentionality." Things are not, in other words, enabled fully to declare themselves as what they truly are until we have turned toward them "intentionally," permitting them thus to step forth out of their amorphous facticity and to disclose their essential qualities.[10]

It was not, of course, a part of Husserl's purpose to offer any defense of distinctively poetic modes of vision and statement. But his distinction between the world as merely perceived and as fully experienced suggests a line of thought whereby a kind of vindication of *poiesis* may be possible. Recent phenomenology, following his lead, maintains not that the fact-world is itself somehow a function of human consciousness but, rather, that it finds its depth of meaning in the intentionality which is brought to it by the human percipient. And it would seem, therefore, that room might be made in cultural experience for poetic "myth," however eccentric or radical it may be, if it does have the effect of permitting the various entities with which we dwell on this earth to stand forth in the clear, bright actuality of their being.

Martin Buber remarks, for example, at a certain point in

10. See Husserl, *Ideas*, passim; see also his *Cartesian Meditations*, trans. Dorion Cairns (The Hague: Martinus Nijhoff, 1960), sec. 14, pp. 31–33.

I and Thou two quite different ways in which we may face a
tree. It may, he suggests, be regarded simply as a stiff column
reared against a background of blue sky and, in the nature
of its leafage and structure, as an example of a certain species;
or we may even "subdue its actual presence and form so
sternly" that it is recognized "only as an expression . . . of the
laws . . . in accordance with which . . . [certain] component sub-
stances mingle and separate." We may, in other words, regard
the tree simply as a phenomenon of the fact-world. But, as
Buber says, we *may* consent to become so "bound up in relation" to this tree before which we stand that it ceases to be
merely an *it*, merely an item of the fact-world, and—being
valued for its own sake, being permitted to "speak," and the
mysterious communication which it bodies forth being "listened to"—becomes a kind of *thou*.[11] Yet there is no question
here of any sort of animism, of the tree being possessed by an
occult power which makes it in some way itself a center of
consciousness. Instead, the mutuality of our relationship with
the tree is wholly grounded in the affectionateness and sympathy with which it is approached, in a delicacy and tact which
permit it to stand forth in the radiant particularity of its
concrete presence. It would be very much like Michelangelo's
"listening" (as Rilke imagined) to the uncut stones, as his
hands caressingly explored their unhewn surfaces in the mo-
ment before the chisel made its first indentation.[12]

So the world "sings" for Theodore Roethke, plants and animals, fire and water, the sun and the moon—indeed, all living
creatures. They sing to one another: they send out their songs
"into the beyond." And it would be only the stupidest sort of
prosaicism which would register any objection to this way of
envisaging what is most primitively marvelous in Creation.
Roethke's hailing the world with song and his listening to the

11. Martin Buber, *I and Thou*, trans. Ronald Gregor Smith (Edin-
burgh: T. & T. Clark, 1937), p. 7.
12. Rainer Maria Rilke, "Of One Who Listened to the Stones," in
Stories of God, trans. M. D. Herter Norton and Nora Purtscher-Wyden-
bruch (New York: W. W. Norton & Co., 1932), pp. 115-21.

melodies which are everywhere to be heard being sung by the
things of earth do not, in other words, present us with another
instance of Ruskin's "pathetic fallacy." For this imagination
of reality as a vast antiphony rests not upon the world's being
invested with human qualities but, rather, upon a lively intuition that both the human and the nonhuman modes of existence are animated and empowered by some primal reality,
which may be denominated simply as Being itself.

This is the *otherness* in which the creatures of earth partic-
ipate, the absolute presence of Being; and it is the genitive
relationship in which all things stand with respect to the Mystery of Being that makes possible the world's great choral
fugue. So, at the dying of the day, when "two wood thrush
sing as one," it is, as Roethke suggests, simply because "Being
delights in being. . . ." Or, as he says in the same poem ("A
Walk in Late Summer," *Words for the Wind*), the "late rose
[that] ravages the casual eye" is nothing other than "a blaze
of being. . . ." And it is the dynamic presence in things of this
primal Leaven that accounts for what happened on the day
when, as the poet says (in "Words for the Wind"),

> I cried, and the birds came down
> And made my song their own.

Now it is this profound and abiding sense in Roethke of all
creaturely existence as instinct with Being which gives to his
poetic persona its predominantly contemplative cast. As he
says in "The Abyss" (*The Far Field*), "Being, not doing, is my
first joy." And it is a morality of contemplation which prompts
him to find something not only maladroit and indelicate but
nearly blasphemous in that rationalist spirit which is so dom-
inated by the intention to bring the world under the reign of
the Idea that, as a consequence, nothing is seen or experienced in the dimension of holiness, or with any reverential
amazement at the way in which—whether it be a garden slug
or a flowing stream or a shock of ragged corn beside a country
road—it is simply steadied and supported by the sheer pres-

ence within it of Being itself. The irritation with which med-
dling intellect is dismissed in "I Cry, Love! Love!" (*Praise to
the End!*) marks a characteristic note:

Reason? That dreary shed, that hutch for grubby schoolboys!
The hedgewren's song says something else.

"Stupor of knowledge lacking inwardness" ("The Pure Fury,"
Words for the Wind) is conceived to be a kind of sickness;
and the poetry expresses, again and again, its desire to "break
through the barrier of rational experience."[13] "O to be delivered from the rational into the realm of pure song," he cries in
"What Can I Tell My Bones?" (*Words for the Wind*).

In one of the late poems, "Infirmity" (*The Far Field*),
Roethke says:

A mind too active is no mind at all;
The deep eye sees the shimmer on the stone. . . .

And the second line does, in a way, summarize a good part of
his testimony. For throughout his life he was committed to an
ocular perspective on reality, feeling that the eye, though it
has sometimes been held to be the "instrument of lechery," is
yet, of all the senses, least drastic in its way of taking hold of
the world. As he said in an early poem, "Prayer" (*Open House*
[1941]):

Its rape is gentle, never more
Violent than a metaphor.

So, since "the Eye's the abettor of / The holiest platonic love,"
he prays that "Light" may "attend" him "to the grave," for
the "deep eye"—which "sees the shimmer on the stone"—
is that faculty which is most adept in helping us to approach the world in what Heidegger would call the spirit of
"letting-be." This it is, indeed, which Roethke considers to be

13. Theodore Roethke, "Comment," in "The Poet and His Critics: A
Symposium," ed. Anthony Ostroff, *New World Writing* (Philadelphia:
J. B. Lippincott Co., 1961), 19 : 214.

the most generous and the most truly human position vis-à-vis our world-environment: it is the attitude of paying heed to "the sigh of what is," of being willing simply to "hum in pure vibration, like a saw," and to marvel at the miraculous way in which things "flame into being." To refuse (again as Heidegger would phrase it) this "releasement toward things" is to condemn oneself to the sterile emptiness of Hell. Thus in the fourth of the "Meditations of an Old Woman":

I think of the self-involved:
The ritualists of the mirror, the lonely drinkers,
The minions of benzedrine and paraldehyde,
And those who submerge themselves deliberately in trivia. . . .

How I wish them awake!
May the high flower of the hay climb into their hearts;
May they lean into light and live;
May they sleep in robes of green, among the ancient ferns;
May their eyes gleam with the first dawn;
May the sun gild them a worm;
May they be taken by the true burning;
May they flame into being!

What one finds, then, as a central quality of Roethke's poetry and a distinctive mark of his basic vision of the world is a profound sense of all earthly reality as invested with a power and presence and as touched by a kind of glory that make it man's principal obligation to offer, in turn, a humble *pietas* as his primary response to the mysteriousness with which all created things reflect the splendid fecundity and holiness of Being. He is a poet who wants very much to exchange (in Camus' phrase) a "smile of complicity" with all the enchantments of the earth, even those belonging to mute, insensate things. He conceives the world to be a place enwrapt in glory, and the reverence which he proposes as a basic norm for human life does, undoubtedly, represent the judgment of an essentially sacramental imagination.

Yet, though the earth itself is such "a tune" as makes him feel the need (in "Four for Sir John Davies") of "a place to sing, and dancing-room," and

> Though dancing needs a master, I had none
> To teach my toes to listen to my tongue.

His confession of being without a dancing-master is Roethke's way of remarking his sense of having nothing but his own unaided imagination to depend upon for reckoning with the ultimate mysteries and astonishments of life. Nor does he misstate his situation here, for he was, most assuredly, a very modern man—in feeling himself to be without any revelation, in feeling himself to be *alone* with the universe and therefore under the necessity himself of building up out of his own experience such coordinating principles as might give coherence and meaning to that experience. Indeed, one feels that it was precisely his sense of being without a "dancing-master" which convinced him that his only chance of finding any order at all lay in listening to his own inner history with the utmost patience and in attempting thereby to repossess his earliest and most primitive encounters with the circumambient world. And it is these researches into the basic material of his own selfhood which are chronicled in his first book, *Open House*, and more crucially in the books of 1948, *The Lost Son and Other Poems*, and 1951, *Praise to the End!*

The record suggests, of course, that the decisive experience in Roethke's early years was his enchantment by the world of his family's greenhouse. He was born (in 1908) and reared in eastern Michigan, in the placid town of Saginaw, where his father and uncle, Otto and Charles Roethke, presided as co-owners over what was then the largest enterprise of its sort in the region; the establishment embraced twenty-five acres within the town, with approximately a quarter of a million feet under glass. The family residences of the two brothers, Otto and Charles, were immediately adjacent to the vast, multistructure, L-shaped nursery, and thus it was the greenhouse

property which made the scene and setting of much of Roethke's childhood play and exploration. Here it was that he early
learned the yearly seasons of this vast conservatory, "which
flowers were planted from seeds, which from slips, which from
bulbs; the various manures and fertilizers in extravagant detail; the flowers' diseases and their cures, . . . the different
periods of growth into maturity, and how fine the timing and
the temperature had to be. . . ."[14]

It was amidst this glassed-in universe of luxuriantly teeming
plant life, as well as in the woods and fields beyond the greenhouse, that Roethke's "vegetal radicalism" (as Kenneth
Burke calls it)[15] doubtless first began to develop. It would appear to have been in this environment, as he studied the minute motions of life in his "narrow vegetable realm" (" 'Long
Live the Weeds,' " *Open House*), that he first began to feel a
"steady storm of correspondences" ("In a Dark Time," *The
Far Field*) between the human and the nonhuman modes of
being, between the life of man and the "minimal" domain of
weeds and flowers, of newts and beetles and all "simple creatures." Thus it was quite early in his life that he decided that
his heart should keep "open house," with "doors . . . widely
swung" before the strangely wondrous "epic of the eyes" presented by the "small things" of the world, even "things un-
holy, marred by curse, / The ugly of the universe."

The poems in *Open House* carry occasional intimations of
this deep sense of relationship and correspondence between
the inner life of the soul and the life of the natural order—as
when, for example, in "The Light Comes Brighter," the coming of spring puts the poet in mind of how

> Soon field and wood will wear an April look,
> The frost be gone. . . .

And soon a branch, part of a hidden scene,

14. Allan Seager, *The Glass House: The Life of Theodore Roethke*
(New York: McGraw-Hill, 1968), p. 21.
15. Kenneth Burke, "The Vegetal Radicalism of Theodore Roethke,"
Sewanee Review 58, no. 1 (January–March 1950): 68–108.

The leafy mind, that long was tightly furled,
Will turn its private substance into green,
And young shoots spread upon our inner world.

But it is in the "greenhouse poems" in *The Lost Son* that we
get the first sustained development of Roethke's vision of the
world as something like Baudelaire's "forest of symbols," as
an order whose things and creatures are not only "in vigorous
communication with one another"[16] but in equally vigorous
communication—or at least in a relationship of reciprocity—
with the human spirit itself. Here it is, as he looks back on
"those fields of glass," that he records how "the whole scheme
of life" was disclosed in his experience of "the natural order
of things." His father was, of course, constantly receiving orders for bouquets and floral arrangements; and he remembers,
for example, something of the pathos that he felt in the cut
flowers, in

> This urge, wrestle, resurrection of dry sticks,
> Cut stems struggling to put down feet,
> What saint strained so much,
> Rose on such lopped limbs to a new life?
>
> ["Cuttings (Later)"]

Or he remembers how

> Bulbs broke out of boxes hunting for chinks in the dark,
> Shoots dangled and drooped,
> . . . .
> And what a congress of stinks!—
> Roots ripe as old bait,
> Pulpy stems, rank, silo-rich,
> Leaf-mould, manure, lime, piled against slippery planks.
> Nothing would give up life:
> Even the dirt kept breathing a small breath.
>
> ["Root Cellar"]

16. Burke, "Vegetal Radicalism of Theodore Roethke," pp. 97–98.

And the poems imply that a formative influence on the boy's deepening awareness of the world was his intuition that this lust for life in dirt and roots and flowers is the same great lust by which the human reality itself is also moved—that, "underground," that same "sucking and sobbing" wherewith plants and flowers struggle to be born are to be heard

> In my veins, in my bones . . .
> The small waters seeping upward,
> The tight grains parting at last.
> When sprouts break out,
> Slippery as fish,
> I quail, lean to beginnings, sheath-wet.
>
> ["Cuttings (Later)"]

But, as the boy assisted his father in the daily labors of their greenhouse, digging away at aggressive weeds,

> Under the concrete benches,
> Hacking at black hairy roots,—. . .
> Digging into the soft rubble underneath,
> Webs and weeds,
> . . . .
> With everything blooming above me,
> Lilies, pale-pink cyclamen, roses,
> Whole fields lovely and inviolate,—
>
> ["Weed Puller"]

what he was most moved by, it seems, was just the stoutness and simplicity with which the little things of the world manage to be what they are. The boy did somehow come to be touched by that most elementary, that most primitive shock—at the fact that there is *something* rather than *nothing*. And the poems in *The Lost Son* record this utter enchantment by things so rudimentary as the bulging of little cells and the search of bulbs for light, the breathing of limply delicate orchids through their "ghostly mouths," "the twittering of swallows above water," or

> the lives on a leaf: the little
> Sleepers, numb nudgers in cold dimensions,
> Beetles in caves, newts, stone-deaf fishes,
> Lice tethered to long limp subterranean weeds,
> Squirmers in bogs,
> And bacterial creepers
> Wriggling through wounds
> Like elvers in ponds,
> Their wan mouths kissing the warm sutures,
> Cleaning and caressing,
> Creeping and healing.
>
>   ["The Minimal"]

Nor do Roethke's "minute particulars run out into great universals" (as it was once said by someone to be the case with Robert Frost's): he has no interest at all in devouring his snails and frogs and slugs and fungi in some system of moralizing analogy. What is truly marvelous is not any message which is conveyed by the "littles" of the world but, rather, simply their showing-forth of Being and of the infinite generosity with which it lets things be. Thus the poems of *The Lost Son* not only utter doxologies in behalf of the amazing songs which are sung by small things; they also honor those who were long ago a part of that greenhouse world and whose gracefulness in relation to its "lovely diminutives" expressed the kind of sanctity which does itself help to keep "creation at ease." The poet remembers, for example, the hands of men who worked for his father—men who were, many of them, cantankerous and full of odd crotchets,[17] but whose hands were a marvel to watch

>   transplanting,
>   Turning and tamping,
>   Lifting the young plants with two fingers,
>   Sifting in a palm-full of fresh loam,—

17. Seager, *Glass House*, p. 13.

One swift movement,—
Then plumping in the bunched roots,
A single twist of the thumbs, a tamping and turning,
All in one. . . .

["Transplanting"]

Or, again, he remembers

That hump of a man bunching chrysanthemums
Or pinching-back asters, or planting azaleas,
Tamping and stamping dirt into pots,—
How he could flick and pick
Rotten leaves or yellowy petals,
Or scoop out a weed close to flourishing roots,
Or make the dust buzz with a light spray,
Or drown a bug in one spit of tobacco juice,
Or fan life into wilted sweet-peas with his hat,
Or stand all night watering roses, his feet blue in rubber boots.

And in one of his most beautiful and moving poems—and one
of the great poems of his career—"Frau Bauman, Frau Schmidt,
and Frau Schwartze," in *The Waking*, he remembers those

three ancient ladies
Who creaked on the greenhouse ladders,
Reaching up white strings
To wind, to wind
The sweet-pea tendrils, the smilax,
Nasturtiums, the climbing
Roses, to straighten
Carnations, red
Chrysanthemums; the stiff
Stems, jointed like corn,
They tied and tucked,—
These nurses of nobody else.
Quicker than birds, they dipped
Up and sifted the dirt;
They sprinkled and shook;

They stood astride pipes,
Their skirts billowing out wide into tents,
Their hands twinkling with wet;
Like witches they flew along rows
Keeping creation at ease;
With a tendril for needle
They sewed up the air with a stem;
They teased out the seed that the cold kept asleep,—
All the coils, loops, and whorls.
They trellised the sun; they plotted for more than themselves.

Which is Roethke's definition of sanctity—plotting for more than oneself, for the care of the good earth, in order that things might simply be what their entelechies intend that they shall be.

The act which is performed, then, by Roethke's early work is an act of anamnesis whereby a poet who conceives himself to be without a "dancing-master" undertakes to lay hold of the most basic certitudes afforded him by his earliest contact with the world. Like the Wordsworth of *The Prelude*, he found those "spots of time, / That with distinct pre-eminence retain / A renovating virtue," to be "moments / . . . taking their date / From our first childhood" (Book 12). For it was then and there—in that lost and far-away vegetal world of his Saginaw childhood—that, as he came to understand, he first learned "to woo the fearful small," to "sing / The soul's immediate joy," and "not to fear infinity, / The far field, the windy cliffs of forever," since all things are gathered together in a great Coinherence in which "everything comes to One, / As we dance on, dance on, dance on"—

> Where ask is have, where seek is find,
> Where knock is open wide.[18]

18. Christopher Smart, *A Song to David*, stanza 77, which supplied Roethke with the title for the opening poem ("Where Knock Is Open Wide") in *Praise to the End!*

Thus, as a result of the investigations recorded in *Open House* and *The Lost Son*, this poet was enabled to discern that, even if "angels are [not] around any more," he might still "say hello to things; / . . . talk to a snail; / . . . see what sings!" Though, to be sure, there was no "dancing-master," he could yet say (in "First Meditation," one of the great poems in *Words for the Wind*):

> In such times, lacking a god,
> I am still happy.

A few weeks after Roethke's death (1 August 1963), John Ciardi, in a memorial piece in the *Saturday Review*, spoke of his verse as "poetry as a medicine man's dance is poetry"[19] —by which he meant to remark a certain incantatory element in Roethke's style. But though Mr. Ciardi's phraseology should be felt to be wildly irrelevant to the early and the late poems, it may not betray many of the poems in the remarkable book of 1951, *Praise to the End!* For, having found in the lost greenhouse-world of his Saginaw Eden the source of those basic certainties which permitted him to be happy while "lacking a god," one feels that in the period immediately following the appearance of *The Lost Son* (1948) Roethke was attempting, indeed, to achieve a kind of total recovery of the childhood experience. And the myriad, evanescent intuitions of childhood are conjured up by means of an incantatory rhetoric so drenched in the "anguish of concreteness" and so radically primitivistic as to make the language of *Praise to the End!* one of the most elusive vocabularies in modern poetry.

The psychologist Jean Piaget suggests that the child's way of taking hold of his world involves a tendency at once to "juxtapose" and to "syncretize" the various items of his experience. That is to say, the child is so enchanted with the

19. John Ciardi, "Theodore Roethke: A Passion and a Maker," *Saturday Review* 46 (31 August 1963): 13.

diversity and multiformity of the world, and his appetite for novelty is so great, that he is not intent on finding principles wherewith to codify and categorize the things and events which come his way. He is content to be nothing more than a connoisseur of the sheer profusion and variousness of reality: instead of attempting to classify things and locate them in some system of order, he simply collects them and holds them in juxtaposition, without much regard for questions of logical propriety. He handles the contents of his experience by way of juxtaposition because he feels that "the world is a wedding" in which everything splays off onto everything else. So his habit of mind is one not only of juxtaposition but also of "syncretism," which Dr. Piaget defines as the

> tendency on the part of children to take things in by means of a comprehensive act of perception instead of by the detection of details, to find immediately and without analysis analogies between words or objects that have nothing to do with each other, to find a reason for every chance event; in a word, it is the tendency to connect everything with everything else.[20]

What is most fundamentally expressed, of course, by the syncretism and juxtaposition of the child's reasoning is a sense of reality in which the subject-object distinction has not yet come to play any decisive part. For, in the earliest period of his life, the child does not say, "I am I, and thou art thou." The world is not yet experienced as a vast not-self, outside and over against one's own being. Instead, everything is experienced, as it were, from the inside: nothing is enclosed within frameworks of identity and causality, and nothing requires mediation, for no distance is felt between ego and world. Normally, it is not until he enters the second or third year of

20. Jean Piaget, *Judgment and Reasoning in the Child* (Paterson, N.J.: Littlefield, Adams & Co., 1964), p. 4.

life that the child begins to deal with reality not merely in the terms of play but also in the terms of inquiry and analysis. Initially, in the earliest stages of his development, he receives the world simply as a marvelous discothèque with whose music he sways, in jubilation and delight and amazement. Now, since it was in this "first" world that Roethke found what it was that had perduringly sustained his life, even in the absence of "a god" or a "dancing-master," the recollective effort, which in his early work had been largely focused on the greenhouse world of his Saginaw childhood, came gradually to broaden out into an attempt at recovering the whole adventure of childhood and the whole evolutionary process whereby the human individual wins the identity of selfhood. And the result of this effort was the astonishing poetry of *Praise to the End!,* whose brilliantly orchestrated chaos (though sometimes defeating for even the most careful reader) represents Roethke's way of miming the primary chaos of psychic life itself.

The title of this book is drawn from a passage in book 1 of *The Prelude,* where Wordsworth says (in the version of 1805–06):

> Praise to the end!
> Thanks likewise for the means! But I believe
> That Nature, oftentimes, when she would frame
> A favor'd Being, from his earliest dawn
> Of infancy doth open out the clouds,
> As at the touch of lightning, seeking him
> With gentlest visitation; not the less,
> Though haply aiming at the self-same end,
> Does it delight her sometimes to employ
> Severer interventions, ministry
> More palpable, and so she dealt with me.

Wordsworth's avowal of the creative role played in the ripening of the self by the adversities and tribulations suffered in one's early years represents precisely the perspective guiding Roethke's own meditation. But his method is hardly Wordsworthian, for the poems of *Praise to the End!* are "all interior drama; no comment; no interpretation,"[21] and it is very clearly "the spring and rush of the child"[22] that he wants to render in these lines from "Where Knock is Open Wide":

> I'm somebody else now.
> Don't tell my hands.
> Have I come to always? Not yet.
> One father is enough.
>
> Maybe God has a house.
> But not here.

—or in the concluding lines of "O Lull Me, Lull Me":

> Soothe me, great groans of underneath,
> I'm still waiting for a foot.
> The poke of the wind's close,
> But I can't go leaping alone.
> For you, my pond,
> Rocking with small fish,
> I'm an otter with only one nose:
> I'm all ready to whistle;
> I'm more than when I was born;
> I could say hello to things;
> I could talk to a snail;
> I see what sings!
> What sings!

The early poems in *Praise to the End!*—such as "Where Knock is Open Wide," "I Need, I Need," and "Bring the Day!" —are written from the standpoint of the child protagonist. The lines are short, and the language is a "dream language"

21. Theodore Roethke, "Open Letter," in *On the Poet and His Craft: Selected Prose of Theodore Roethke,* ed. Ralph J. Mills, Jr. (Seattle: University of Washington Press, 1965), p. 41.
22. Ibid.

that so mingles the material of nursery rhyme and childish fancy as to convey a direct impression of the inwardness of the child's *Lebenswelt*. Roethke felt that

> in this kind of poem, the poet, in order to be true to what is most universal in himself, should not rely on allusion; should not comment or employ many judgment words; should not meditate (or maunder). He must scorn being "mysterious" or loosely oracular, but be willing to face up to genuine mystery. His language must be compelling and immediate: he must create an actuality. He must be able to telescope image and symbol, if necessary, without relying on the obvious connectives: to speak in a kind of psychic shorthand when his protagonist is under great stress. He must be able to shift his rhythms rapidly. . . . He works intuitively. . . .[23]

It is this aesthetic which is controlling the first of the two parts of the book, where the poetry is rendering that jumbled and irregular landscape of the fledgling whose identity is still in process of formation. And the drama which these poems reflect is that which Jung took to be the essence of the child's adventure—"the conquest of the dark,"[24] the journey from the night of unconsciousness into the day of awareness and comprehension. As it is said in the beautiful exclamation with which "Bring the Day!" closes:

> O small bird wakening,
> Light as a hand among blossoms,
> Hardly any old angels are around any more.
> The air's quiet under the small leaves.
> The dust, the long dust, stays.
> The spiders sail into summer.
> It's time to begin!
> To begin!

23. Ibid., p. 42.
24. Carl G. Jung, *Psyche and Symbol* (New York: Doubleday, 1958), p. 131.

Part 2 of *Praise to the End!* is comprised of the series of poems which had concluded *The Lost Son* ("The Lost Son," "The Long Alley," "A Field of Light," "The Shape of the Fire") and three others—"Praise to the End!," "Unfold! Unfold!," and "I Cry, Love! Love!" Here the journey begun in Part 1—in search of identity and selfhood—is continued, but, the protagonist being now older, the prevailing emphasis falls more heavily on those "severer interventions" (as Wordsworth calls them) which are employed by the executive powers to "frame / A favor'd Being." "The Lost Son," which makes one of the crucial statements in this whole group of poems, places its opening scene in a cemetery:

> At Woodlawn I heard the dead cry:
> I was lulled by the slamming of iron,
> A slow drip over stones,
> Toads brooding in wells.
> All the leaves stuck out their tongues;
> I shook the softening chalk of my bones. . . .

And the pilgrim's journey, as it is traced out in this second part of the book, seems often to be along the dark underside of things—the disquiet aroused by the dead father's ghost, the unease consequent upon sexual sins and alienations, the dismay provoked by an industrial society's desecration of air and water and earth, the haunting awareness of death as the ultimate and unavoidable emergency of life. So it comes to be that, for the lost son, there is no dodging the question:

> Which is the way I take;
> Out of what door do I go,
> Where and to whom?

Always, however, the basic order of perception is that which has been found to be the determining framework of Roethke's vision—namely, the sense of the human situation as, most fundamentally, one of our simply standing (as Heidegger would say) in-the-neighborhood-of-Being, in the outright *presence* of that-which-is. The gesture which his poetry performs is a gesture of *Gelassenheit*, of abandonment, of surrender to the sheer presence of Being in the things and creatures of earth. For this poet, as he recalls in "Unfold! Unfold!" was

> privy to oily fungus and the algae of standing waters;
> Honored . . . by the ancient fellowship of rotten stems.

So he says (in "A Field of Light"):

> Listen, love,
> The fat lark sang in the field;
> I touched the ground, the ground warmed by the killdeer,
> The salt laughed and the stones;
> The ferns had their ways, and the pulsing lizards,
> And the new plants, still awkward in their soil,
> The lovely diminutives.
> I could watch! I could watch!
> I saw the separateness of all things!
> My heart lifted up with the great grasses;
> The weeds believed me, and the nesting birds.
> There were clouds making a rout of shapes crossing a
>   windbreak of cedars,
> And a bee shaking drops from a rain-soaked honeysuckle.
> The worms were delighted as wrens.
> And I walked, I walked through the light air;
> I moved with the morning.

In February of 1963, just a few months before his death—in a statement prepared for a public forum at Northwestern University that is often astonishing in the naked simplicity of his self-revelation—Roethke asserted his belief that "everything that lives is holy" and declared the governing intention of his art to be that of invoking "these holy forms of life." "One could even put this," he said, "theologically: St. Thomas says, 'God is above all things by the excellence of His nature; nevertheless, He is in all things as causing the being of all

things.' "[25] Therefore, Roethke concluded, such a poetry as
his own, in calling upon snails and weeds and nesting birds
and all the various "lovely diminutives" of the world, is indeed
calling upon God. And it is this persuasion, it is this faith, that
constitutes the vital center of Roethke's vision.

His poetry, however, is to be found speaking only very
rarely of God, and never in the accents of any sort of mystical
religion. He was a man who had no desire to transcend the
finites and definites that make up the common occasions of
life; his poetry is uninfluenced by any great lust for infinities
and eternities. Nor was he a poet of Supreme Fictions, and he
seems never to have had any impulse to make such a claim
as Stevens':

> Out of my mind the golden ointment rained,
> And my ears made the flowing hymns they heard.
> I was myself the compass of that sea:
>
> I was the world in which I walked, and what I saw
> Or heard or felt came not but from myself;
> And there I found myself more truly and more strange.[26]

On the contrary, it was in the world of the actual—established,
as he felt it to be, independently of the human intelligence—
that Roethke found his house of prayer. But it was a house of
prayer, and he was no mere "facer of facts," of facts which say
only "that nothing much can come out of our reality."[27] For
he found an engrossing but unfathomable density in the Is-
ness of everything that exists, in the mysterious munificence
with which even dirt and weeds and garden slugs are indwelt
by Being. So his characteristic mode of predication is not the
subjunctive or the imperative but the indicative, and it is his

25. Theodore Roethke, "On 'Identity,'" *On the Poet and His Craft*,
pp. 24–25. This paper was originally presented at Northwestern as part
of a panel discussion devoted to the theme of "Identity."
26. Wallace Stevens, "Tea at the Palaz of Hoon," in *The Collected
Poems of Wallace Stevens* (New York: Alfred A. Knopf, 1955), p. 65.
27. William F. Lynch, S.J., *Christ and Apollo: The Dimensions of
the Literary Imagination* (New York: Sheed and Ward, 1960), p. 11.

astonishment and wonder—at the marvelous fecundity and amplitude of Being wherewith the things of earth are steadied and exalted, and by which they manage to last. As Tony Tanner was reminding us in his book of 1965, *The Reign of Wonder*, it is precisely in this order of perception that American literature has very often found its central commitment. For whether one turns to Emerson or to Mark Twain, to Thoreau or to Gertrude Stein, to Whitman or to William Carlos Williams, to Henry James or to Hemingway, what one finds being constantly stressed is

> the radical importance of a true way of seeing; the generous, open, even naive, undulled and reverent eye—as opposed to the self-interested squinting and peering of the greedy utilitarian social eye, and the cold myopia of the scientific, analytic eye. Their ideal is an eye of passive wonder.[31]

Judgment, says the narrator of Saul Bellow's *Dangling Man*, is "second to wonder"—which neatly summarizes what has tended to be a major premise of the American imagination, that the first and most proper response to be offered the world is one of simple marveling at the variousness and multiplicity of its enchantments.

But Roethke deserves to be considered deeply American not only in his commitment to wonder as a primary mode of vision, but also in his conformity to Carlyle's portrayal of Emerson as "a *Soliloquizer* on the eternal mountain-tops only, in vast solitudes where men and their affairs all lie hushed in a very dim remoteness; and only *the man* and the stars and the earth are visible."[32] The tendency of our literature to be suspicious of social reality and to find its ballast in what Emerson called "the simple genuine self against the whole world" has, of course, been often noted, and there is no gain-

31. Tony Tanner, *The Reign of Wonder: Naivety and Reality in American Literature* (Cambridge: Cambridge University Press, 1965), p. 355.

32. Quoted ibid., p. 9, from *Selections from Ralph Waldo Emerson: An Organic Anthology*, ed. Stephen Whicher (Cambridge, Mass.: Houghton Mifflin Co., 1957), p. 492.

saying that it marks a deeply settled habit of thought among our classic writers of both the nineteenth and the twentieth centuries. "Of the great formative works of the American imagination one is set on a river (*Huckleberry Finn*), one on an open road (*Song of Myself*), one on the sea (*Moby Dick*), . . . one by a pond (*Walden*)."[33] And many of the most exemplary personages—Ahab, Hester Prynne, Huck Finn, Nick Adams, Isaac McCaslin, Jack Burden, and Eugene Henderson —are fugitives from society. Fitzgerald tells us that "out of the corner of his eye Gatsby saw that the blocks of the sidewalk really formed a ladder and mounted to a secret place above the trees—he could climb to it, if he climbed alone, and once there he could . . . gulp down the incomparable milk of wonder." And it is toward such a point, above the flurry of the human City—"where men and their affairs all lie hushed in a very dim remoteness"—that our literature often seems to have been aiming.

Now Theodore Roethke's poetic personality is very much that of an *isolé*, and in this also, surely, he may be felt to be a thoroughly American poet. He does, of course, admit into his poetry a number of very remarkable personages—some of whom are identified and others of whom are without name— such as his mother and father, his sister, his Aunt Tilly, his Uncle Charles, "the three ancient ladies / Who creaked on the greenhouse ladders," various "chums" of childhood, and the old woman listening "to the weeds' vesperal whine" as her life draws to a close. But, though his poetry by no means expresses a vision that is bluntly or complacently egocentric, Roethke seems never to have found any high significance in the realm of what Martin Buber calls "the interhuman" or to have believed that "it is from one man to another that the heavenly bread of self-being is passed."[34] The ontological mystery was not for him a preeminently human mystery, and

---

33. Tanner, *Reign of Wonder*, p. 337.
34. See Martin Buber, *The Knowledge of Man*, trans. Maurice Friedman and Ronald Gregor Smith (New York: Harper and Row, 1965), pp. 72–88, 71.

the dialogical drama of our human togetherness did not constitute for him the essential medium or agency through which the self encounters Being. The famous line from Auden's poem "September 1, 1939" —"We must love one another or die"—makes a kind of announcement which is in no way of a piece with the basic stress of Roethke's poetry. For though he loved, as he said, what "is near at hand, / Always, in earth and air," it seems that the tensions and fulfillments that make up our human sociality were never felt to be quite so near at hand as sprouting bulbs and wriggling worms, as sighing weeds and the "midnight eyes" of all the little creatures of the earth. He could join the Yeats who listened to the "sweet everlasting Voices" which "call in birds, in wind on the hill, / In shaken boughs, in tide on the shore."[35] But there was another Yeats, whose mind and art moved in a dimension altogether beyond Roethke— the Yeats, for example, who prefaced the following lines with an epigraph from Thomas Mann which says that "In our time the destiny of man presents its meaning in political terms":

> How can I, that girl standing there,
> My attention fix
> On Roman or on Russian
> Or on Spanish politics?
> Yet here's a travelled man that knows
> What he talks about,
> And there's a politician
> That has read and thought,
> And maybe what they say is true
> Of war and war's alarms. . . .[36]

"Ye littles, lie more close!" says Roethke in the poem "In Evening Air" (*The Far Field*); and this "minimalism," which is recurrently echoed throughout his work, does unfortunately

35. William Butler Yeats, "The Everlasting Voices," *The Collected Poems of W. B. Yeats* (New York: Macmillan, 1951), p. 53.
36. William Butler Yeats, "Politics," *Collected Poems*, p. 337.

have the effect of shutting out large tracts of experience—
nearly all those regions in which "the destiny of man presents
its meaning in political terms," in the terms of our life *together* in the human *Polis*. The fact of the matter is that he
was a man "more responsive to intimations of being when they
offer themselves in plants than in people,"[37] so that finally, in
his vast solitudes, men and their affairs do lie all too hushed,
in a very dim remoteness indeed. And the result is an impov-
erishment, a failure to carry the sacramental principle to its
full and decisive limit.

But, however sparsely populated Roethke's universe may be,
at least lovers are not excluded; and the love poems in *Words
for the Wind* and *The Far Field* belong, many of them, among
the great modern triumphs in this genre, with the finest lyrics
of Yeats and Graves and Auden. Here again, as at so many
other points in his poetry, we see how thoroughly unplatonic
was the essential cast of Roethke's mind, for what he values in
heterosexual love is not some ethereal felicity to which it
gives access, not some pallid empyrean into which it leads: on
the contrary, it is the riot and romp and frolic of sexual joy
that he celebrates, and the poetry sounds a pure hosanna in
behalf of the fleshly delights of the partnership between man
and woman. The poem entitled "Words for the Wind" closes,
for example, with the following lines:

> I kiss her moving mouth,
> Her swart hilarious skin;
> She breaks my breath in half;
> She frolicks like a beast;
> And I dance round and round,
> A fond and foolish man,
> And see and suffer myself
> In another being, at last.

Or again, the second stanza of "I Knew a Woman" says:

37. Donoghue, "Roethke's Broken Music," p. 144.

> How well her wishes went! She stroked my chin,
> She taught me Turn, and Counter-turn, and Stand;
> She taught me Touch, that undulant white skin;
> I nibbled meekly from her proffered hand;
> She was the sickle; I, poor I, the rake,
> Coming behind her for her pretty sake
> (But what prodigious mowing we did make).

And it is a similar reveling in the joyous privilege of sensuality which the love poems express again and again. "We did not fly the flesh. Who does, when young?" Roethke's candor about the itch of desire is unsullied by any smirking embarrassment or uneasiness of conscience, and his exuberance gives to the rhetoric of his love poetry a fervency and an eloquence that make it something very remarkable indeed.

It would be, however, a miscalculation to conceive the love poems as dedicated to nothing more than the careless raptures of sensual joy. For, despite all their rollicking carnality, they carry a larger freight of meaning. One clue to this additional dimension is given in the beautifully executed cycle of poems entitled "Four for Sir John Davies" which appeared in *The Waking* and was reissued in *Words for the Wind*. It is "The Dance," the first poem in the sequence, which is perhaps most heavily dependent on Roethke's reading of Sir John Davies, for this minor English poet of the sixteenth century, in the long poem *Orchestra* (1594), was proposing that the harmonious interrelationships among the various realms of Being are conceivable as all comprising a sort of cosmic dance in which the whole of reality participates. It is this notion which activates the meditation recorded in the opening poem of Roethke's cycle, where he wonders if this metaphor retains any relevance for the modern imagination:

> Is that dance slowing in the mind of man
> That made him think the universe could hum?

But, as for himself, he seems to be saying, the "great wheel" continues to turn, and he likens the clumsiness of his own dancing to the ungainly romping of a bear. "Though dancing needs a master, I had none / To teach my toes to listen to my tongue." Yet, even so, "I was dancing-mad, and how / That came to be the bears and Yeats would know."

To dance, however, one needs a partner; and so, in the second poem of the sequence ("The Partner"), the poet is joined by a woman (who "would set sodden straw on fire"). The form of his dance now becomes that of sexual union:

> We played a measure with commingled feet:
> The lively dead had taught us to be fond.
> ·
> Light altered light along the living ground.
> She kissed me close, and then did something else.
> My marrow beat as wildly as my pulse.

And, in the last line of the poem, these two are playing "in that dark world where gods have lost their way." Here, immediately, we feel a new seriousness, for this "dark world" is presumably the world where Sir John Davies' cosmic dance begins now to be "slowing in the mind of man" because no dancing-master is to be found. Roethke seems to be suggesting that what the protagonist and his companion have together is that which will alone make this darkness tolerable.

Indeed, what is only hinted at in the closing lines of "The Partner" is made quite explicit in the opening lines of the following poem ("The Wraith"), where Roethke says:

> Incomprehensible gaiety and dread
> Attended what we did. Behind, before,
> Lay all the lonely pastures of the dead;
> The spirit and the flesh cried out for more.
> We two, together, on a darkening day
> Took arms against our own obscurity.

This makes as plain a declaration as is to be found anywhere in Roethke's love poems of what he considers to be the true office of love. It is, he intends to say, our best, perhaps our only, way of taking arms against our frailty, our "obscurity," our defenselessness before the infinite hazards to which man is exposed. It is our way of ringing ourselves round with a campfire that staves off the environing dark of the nighttime wilderness looming beyond. But the lines which immediately follow this stanza may remind us how inappropriate it would be to take what Roethke is saying here as his conception of the "spiritual" meaning of love. For, even as the cycle deepens down into the "dark world where gods have lost their way," the actual physicality of human love remains the primary datum of the poem:

> Did each become the other in that play?
> She laughed me out, and then she laughed me in;
> In the deep middle of ourselves we lay;
> When glory failed, we danced upon a pin.

Sexuality is not, in other words, merely a metaphor whereby one speaks of the really important thing, which is something "spiritual." For (unlike Shelley) Roethke never conceives felicity to be any sort of "unbodied joy," and his love poetry is always fully committed to the claims of the flesh. But, there, the stress of body against body casts a spell wherewith, as he says in the concluding poem of the cycle ("The Vigil"), "We undid chaos" and "mocked before the black / And shapeless night that made no answer back."

It is this whole undercurrent of meaning in the love poems which leads on into what increasingly became one of Roethke's major concerns in the final years of his life—namely, the last great emergency that a man faces, which is none other than the certain eventuality of death. For even those lovers who are most intensely involved in each other's lives are, as it were, only pawing the dark,[38] as Roethke very clearly wants to say

38. See Theodore Roethke, "The Renewal," *Words for the Wind*: "I know I love, yet know not where I am; / I paw the dark, the shifting midnight air."

in one of his most memorable poems, "The Sensualists"
(*Words for the Wind*), which deserves to be quoted in full:

> "There is no place to turn," she said,
>   "You have me pinned so close;
> My hair's all tangled on your head,
>   My back is just one bruise;
> I feel we're breathing with the dead;
>   O angel, let me loose!"
>
> And she was right, for there beside
>   The gin and cigarettes,
> A woman stood, pure as a bride,
>   Affrighted from her wits,
> And breathing hard, as that man rode
>   Between those lovely tits.
>
> "My shoulder's bitten from your teeth;
>   What's that peculiar smell?
> No matter which one is beneath,
>   Each is an animal,"—
> The ghostly figure sucked its breath,
>   And shuddered toward the wall;
> Wrapped in the tattered robe of death,
>   It tiptoed down the hall.
>
> "The bed itself begins to quake,
>   I hate this sensual pen;
> My neck, if not my heart, will break
>   If we do this again,"—
> Then each fell back, limp as a sack,
>   Into the world of men.

Here Roethke offers, through the drama of his poem, a kind
of evidence of how impossible it is, finally, for love effectively
to confer anything like the sort of final solace which Matthew
Arnold's "Dover Beach" envisages. For, after its ecstasy, the

lovers must fall "back . . . / Into the world of men"—the "dark world," where one cannot avoid the disquieting chill of "the shifting midnight air." "All sensual love's but dancing on a grave" ("The Dying Man," *Words for the Wind*).

In the great sequence of poems which concludes *Words for the Wind*, "Meditations of an Old Woman," the protagonist is one who has felt the frosty touch of "the shifting midnight air." So, in the "late afternoon" of her life, after long years of yearning "for absolutes that never come," she is unprepared to give any quick assent to Eliot's assurance in "Little Gidding" that

> All shall be well, and
> All manner of thing shall be well.

For, as she says,

> It is difficult to say all things are well,
> When the worst is about to arrive. . . .

She is a woman who has journeyed far—"into the waste lonely places / Behind the eye; the lost acres at the edge of smoky cities." But a lifetime's effort is without any crown, and

> On love's worst ugly day,
> The weeds hiss at the edge of the field,
> The small winds make their chilly indictments.

As she draws "near the graves of the great dead," she wonders what she can tell her bones. It is a profoundly poignant drama of self-interrogation and search that the five poems making up the cycle create. But these "Meditations" do not move toward the embrace of a resurrection-faith. Instead, the old woman says (in "Her Becoming"), "I have learned to sit quietly"—which is to say that she has learned (as Roethke puts it in one of the poems in *The Far Field*, "The Abyss") to "wait, unafraid, beyond the fearful instant."

This is, indeed, the essential *action* in the poems in which she figures, an action of meditation and of waiting. As Roethke says in one of his late poems, "The Right Thing" (*The Far Field*), "Let others probe the mystery if they can." But the ancient lady of the "Meditations" is no longer a "time-harried prisoner of *Shall* and *Will*": she has learned to prefer "the still joy," to listen to a "snail's music"—and simply to wait. To be sure, as she says, "in the days of my slowness . . . / I've become a strange piece of flesh," infirm and "whiskery." But, as she declares in the great final lines of the "First Meditation," even "lacking a god, / I am still happy." For there is to be heard the call of

> The cerulean, high in the elm,
> Thin and insistent as a cicada,
> And the far phoebe, singing,
> The long plaintive notes floating down,
> Drifting through leaves, oak and maple,
> Or the whippoorwill, along the smoky ridges. . . .

And thus, even as one faces the last great extremity of life, a certain nonchalance or poise is possible. "Birds are around," mice are still capering in the straw, stones can still be caressed; and the old woman has come to believe that there is "wisdom in objects," for the speech that passes between birds and trees, between salmon and shallow streams, between sun and earth is a speech that testifies of the presence of Being beneath and above and in all the things and creatures of this world. So, she says, "I become the wind" and "recover my tenderness by long looking."

Indeed, it is very much in this way that the disquiet aroused by the prospect of death is finally allayed in many of the remarkable poems making up Roethke's posthumous volume, *The Far Field*—in the poems forming the cycle called "North American Sequence," in "The Abyss," and in several of the magnificent poems belonging to the "Sequence, Sometimes Metaphysical" ("In Evening Air," "Infirmity," "The Right Thing," "Once More, the Round"). They all tend to reach a similar conclusion—that, baffling and fearful as the thought of death may be, once the spirit gathers itself together to "em-

brace the world," it will find itself no longer fearing "infinity, /
The far field, the windy cliffs of forever," since when one
breathes

> with the birds,
> The spirit of wrath becomes the spirit of blessing,
> And the dead begin from their dark to sing. . . .

Thus it is that the poet comes upon "the true ease of myself"
and unlearns "the lingo of exasperation"—by not insisting
upon too much reality (which "can be a dazzle, a surfeit")
and by simply faring-forth into the things of earth which do
themselves, for all their finitude (as "The Fair Field" says),
"reveal infinitude."

On days of mottled clouds, of thinly misted mornings or
evenings, we may still "rock between dark and dark," waiting
for God. But there is one deeply felt intuition on which Roethke's entire poetry is built—that, miraculously, the universe in
which we dwell is so ordered that Being never deserts the
things and creatures of earth, that it bestows itself upon them
with a most handsome munificence, and that, even when we
must wait "in a dark time" for the gods, a man need not "out-
leap the sea— / The edge of all the land"—in order to dis-
cover that in himself by which he is steadied and "in which all
creatures share. . . ." In short, even in the darkest time, a man
can still say (as in "The Abyss"):

> I receive! I have been received!
> I hear the flowers drinking in their light,
> I have taken counsel of the crab and the sea-urchin,
> I recall the falling of small waters,
> The stream slipping beneath the mossy logs,
> Winding down to the stretch of irregular sand,
> The great logs piled like matchsticks.
>
> I am most immoderately married:
> . . . .
>
> Being . . . is my first joy.

So this poet was one who could say, with enormous gusto and conviction, "I count myself among the happy poets."[39] He adored his life "with the Bird, the abiding Leaf, / With the Fish, the questing Snail," and he wanted to "dance with William Blake / For love, for Love's sake. . . ." One of the lines in his poem "I Cry, Love! Love!" declares: "I proclaim once more a condition of joy." And this was an abiding intention of his verse, to proclaim a condition of joy. For, despite his recurrent bouts with a most baffling and often humiliating mental illness,[40] he was indeed a happy poet. So the cadence which his poetry sounds, with a deeply moving kind of repetitiveness and with an eloquence unique in the literature of modern poetry, is that of reverence for life—and of thanksgiving:

> I could watch! I could watch!
> I saw the separateness of all things!
> My heart lifted up with the great grasses;
> . . . .
> And I walked, I walked through the light air;
> I moved with the morning.

And there is perhaps no other passage in the whole of Roethke's poetry that more beautifully expresses his distinctive *pietas* than the great exclamation with which "The Shape of the Fire" (*Praise to the End!*) closes:

> To have the whole air!
> The light, the full sun

39. Roethke, "Open Letter," p. 40.

40. Roethke held a professorship in the department of English of the University of Washington (Seattle) from 1948 until his death in 1963, and the explanation offered by his friend and colleague Robert Heilman (then chairman of the department) in January of 1959 to the vice-president of the university as to why Roethke frequently required "leaves" for illness gives a sufficient statement of his problem: "Roethke has a nervous ailment of the 'manic-depressive' type. Periodically he goes into a 'high' or 'low' state in which he is incapable of teaching. It is in such periods that he has been on sick leave." Professor Heilman's letter —a moving document—is quoted in full in Seager, *Glass House*, pp. 253–56.

Coming down on the flowerheads,
The tendrils turning slowly,
A slow snail-lifting, liquescent;
To be by the rose
Rising slowly out of its bed,
Still as a child in its first loneliness;
To see cyclamen veins become clearer in early sunlight,
And mist lifting out of the brown cattails;
To stare into the after-light, the glitter left on the lake's
   surface,
When the sun has fallen behind a wooden island;
To follow the drops sliding from a lifted oar,
Held up, while the rower breathes, and the small boat drifts
   quietly shoreward;
To know that light falls and fills, often without our knowing,
As an opaque vase fills to the brim from a quick pouring,
Fills and trembles at the edge yet does not flow over,
Still holding and feeding the stem of the contained flower.

Here, then, is an American poet of our time immensely eligible for inclusion among the major poets using the English language in this century and one who, for all the modernity of his independence of any established tradition of religious belief, presents one of the great examples in recent literature of a sacramental conception of the world. Roethke's way of developing the logic of "sacramentation" may, of course, be felt not to have pressed quite far enough, for, as we have remarked, his is a sacramental vision that appears to have been somewhat more at home with the nonhuman than with the human modes of reality. And thus he may need, as it were, to be completed by the kinds of insights in which poets like William Carlos Williams and W. H. Auden and Robert Penn Warren and Richard Wilbur have specialized. Yet he managed to win the firmest kind of grip on what is of the very essence of the sacramental principle—namely, that nothing may be a sacrament unless everything is, at bottom, sacramental, and that ours may be considered to be a sacramental universe because, in its every aspect and dimension, it is instinct with that which appears to be *for* man rather than *against* him—which is none other than Being itself.

So he is a poet who brings us back into "proximity to the Source"; and his legacy deserves to be accorded a very large place, most especially in a period so distinguished as ours by a great yearning to find the world's "otherness" grounded in some real dialectic of reciprocity—because our world is indwelt by grace and holiness and is therefore under the law of participation. He is, in short, a poet a part of whose competence it may be to guide the spirit and to instruct the imagination of such people as ourselves, who seem frequently today to be engaged in a new search for the possibility of conceiving the world to be a truly sacramental reality.

Bibliographical Note: Works by Theodore Roethke

Open House. New York: Alfred A. Knopf, 1941.

The Lost Son and Other Poems. Garden City, N.Y.: Doubleday and Co., 1948.

Praise to the End! Garden City, N.Y.: Doubleday and Co., 1951.

The Waking: Poems, 1933–1953. Garden City, N.Y.: Doubleday and Co., 1953.

Words for the Wind: The Collected Verse of Theodore Roethke. Garden City, N.Y.: Doubleday and Co., 1958.

I Am! Says the Lamb. Garden City, N.Y.: Doubleday and Co., 1961.

Sequence, Sometimes Metaphysical. Iowa City, Iowa: The Stone Wall Press, 1963.

The Far Field. Garden City, N.Y.: Doubleday and Co., 1964.

The Collected Poems of Theodore Roethke. Garden City, N.Y.: Doubleday and Co., 1966.

On the Poet and His Craft: Selected Prose of Theodore Roethke. Edited by Ralph J. Mills, Jr. Seattle: University of Washington Press, 1965.

Selected Letters of Theodore Roethke. Edited by Ralph J. Mills, Jr. Seattle: University of Washington Press, 1968.

Index